MIGHTIER THAN THE SWORD

Edited by Donna Samworth

First published in Great Britain in 2012 by:
Forward Poetry
Remus House
Coltsfoot Drive
Peterborough
PE2 9BF
Telephone: 01733 890099
Website: www.forwardpoetry.co.uk

Book Design by Spencer Hart & Tim Christian

SB ISBN 978-1-84418-609-9

FOREWORD

In 2009, Poetry Rivals was launched. It was one of the biggest and most prestigious competitions ever held by Forward Poetry. Due to the popularity and success of this talent contest like no other, we have taken Poetry Rivals into 2012, where it has proven to be even bigger and better than previous years.

Poets of all ages and from all corners of the globe were invited to write a poem that showed true creative talent - a poem that would stand out from the rest.

We are proud to present the resulting anthology, an inspiring collection of verse carefully selected by our team of editors. Reflecting the vibrancy of the modern poetic world, it is brimming with imagination and diversity.

As well as encouraging creative expression, Poetry Rivals has also given writers a vital opportunity to showcase their work to the public, thus providing it with the wider audience it so richly deserves.

THE POEMS

PROBLEMS FACED BY GIRLS

A girl a major problem
This is what the society believes in
The girl, a cause of loss to the family
Though, she's trying to last.

She sits alone and moans,
She wants to help but she doesn't ask
People find it a great task,
There is no life, deep in her heart.

The girl doesn't believe in fate
She's all alone without a mate
She's broken, she's shattered,
She has no way to lay or stay.

She's hurt inside
There's no one to talk to
They say, 'Oh she's to be blamed,'
But they don't know what she's going through.

She goes to bed crying
And wakes up to a whole new day
Hoping it will be better,
But finds out it's still the same.

She wants love
She wants care
No one to share,
That's all she can say.

The day has arrived
It's now time to decide
Still no rays of hope to be seen
She makes up her mind and chooses suicide.

Femida Osman Sattar

MOTHERS AND DAUGHTERS - A RELATIONSHIP TO BE TREASURED

Our daughters are the most precious of our treasures
Daughters are the brightest star glimmering in the sky
They are the silver lining on those dark black cloudy days
They are a wonder, sweetness, joy and a lifetime's delight.

Mothers are their daughter's role model
Their sacrifices made through the year will always be grateful
A mother's love for her daughters is beyond drudgery circumstances
She is the only person who could be relied on the things that matter the most of all.

Mothers and daughters are suspended, a loving eye to eye embrace
A daughter is a mother's gender partner, her closest ally in the family
The mother's presence is like a fixed light
That gives the daughter the security to move out safely
Mothers and daughter never really part . . . bound in the beating of each other's heart.

Sabrin Osman Sattar

FANTASY

In clandestine reverie,
You belong to me.
Your hand in mine,
Your heart is kind.
We race to the sun,
Our forever has begun.
This radiant future beam . . .
One lovely perfect dream.

Diana Kwiatkowski Rubin

LAST DAYS COMING

Soon I'll be turning a new page
I will be pensionable age
Don't know what to think or say
But I look forward to the day
What I'll do I don't know
I believe I have a lot to show
Carry on the best I can
Don't feel like an old man
Some friends go for a walk
Or just sit and talk
I like to go to the pub
Get a pint and nice bit of grub
Sit in the park in the sun
Watching the kids having fun
Not much more I can say
I just live from day to day.

Frank Tonner

REBIRTH

Each night I go to sleep and die
Morning awakes me from night's death
Like emerging light beneath tarnished silver

Light edging the beginning of each day
Yesterday's sunset gone, wine spent embers
With this new day's brilliance – a serpent of eternity

Unfurling its coil somewhere to the baby's kick
Beneath the hump, or an unfurling bud
Stretched in celebration at the transformation

Of chrysalis to butterfly,
Winged in its constancy
Of re-enactment and rebirth.

John Greeves

TITANIC

I was there on the great Titanic,
I stood on its sweeping decks,
And looked over the vast Atlantic
That covers so many wrecks.
She was the newest and finest ship,
Owned by the White Star Line.
And was making her first ever trip,
As I was making the first of mine.
The passenger list included the names
Of some of the wealthiest in the land.
And though I didn't recognise some of the names,
I could see they were all very grand.
The nights were cold, the stars were bright,
The breath from my mouth like steam
And the throb of the engines in the night,
Was the music in my dreams
By day in a deckchair I took my ease,
As I listened to the band.
And all the while the grey-green sea
Held a promise in its hand.
To take me to a brave new world,
Far from my place of birth.
Where I would see my plans unfurled,
And some day I would prove my worth.
In the evenings, 'neath huge chandeliers,
I dined with the crème de la crème.
And though they were never my peers,
I could pretend I was one of them.
The band was playing brightly,
And I sat there in that future tomb,
Which I had done almost nightly,
As we sailed towards our doom.
I watched my fellow passengers
Lifting their glasses to drink,
All aware of the messengers
Forging their ship to ship link.
Warning of icebergs along their route,
Out there in the North Atlantic.
From the steerage deck came the sound of a flute,
And the music became more frantic,
The people were having a 'shindig'
And they danced to an Irish tune,
Whirling round and round in a manic jig,
As the merry sound filled the room.

And all the while they were unknowing,
Of the fate that awaited them all,
That the danger from icebergs was growing,
And though the wireless picked up the call,
It was almost ignored 'til too late,
And out there in the cold dark sea,
Was the 'berg that would seal our fate.
There was no indication, no swell in the sea,
So no froth at the iceberg's base.
And with no binoculars to aid his sight,
And the bitter cold striking his face,
The lookout saw a mass loom out of the night.
And three rings he gave on the warning bell.
That meant 'object directly ahead!'
Then down the bridge phone, he gave a great yell.
'Iceberg ahead sir! Iceberg ahead!'
First Officer Murdoch said, 'Turn to port!'
But the ship was going too fast.
And the space between iceberg and ship too short.
So the die was already cast.
Though they avoided a head on collision,
A spur caught through the ship's side like a knife.
And within a few hours there came the decision,
'To the lifeboats!' but no husband could go with his wife.
Only mothers and children, or women alone,
There wouldn't be enough lifeboats to carry them all,
So not many would live to go home.
Meanwhile people slept, or sat drinking a nightcap,
As the tragedy began to unfold.
They were rudely awakened by the steward's loud rap,
And ordered out on the decks bitter cold.
Afraid and bewildered they said to each other,
'This ship is completely unsinkable.'
A child's crying was hushed by its mother,
Whilst she tried not to think the unthinkable
I had been playing cards when disaster struck,
As the ice sliced through Titanic's side.
I was just beginning to have some luck,
But at the moment my luck died.
The actual encounter was not felt by all,
And they wondered, 'Why all the fuss?'
But later as they watched the great funnel fall,
They were praying, 'My God, please save us'.
The radio gave out urgent calls of distress
And flares were sent into the sky.
Yet a nearby ship didn't rightly assess,

The flares of an SOS cry.
They thought they were part of a celebration,
And so didn't come to our aid.
They completely misread our situation.
As we watched their bright lights fade.
The engines had stopped, the lower decks flooded,
The flute and the fiddle were stilled.
Sometimes a body, its head and face bloodied,
Floated by, adding a chill to the already chilled.
Captain Smith said, 'Take to the lifeboats!'
But there weren't enough lifeboats for all,
I thought *I'll find something that floats*,
As I watched the start of another brawl.
The role of the sea has always been,
That women and children come first
But as terror and panic painted the scene,
I saw mankind at its very worst,
As they desperately fought for the chance to survive.
And as I watched all the boats quickly fill,
I knew I would be lucky to end up alive.
Husbands said their weary 'goodbyes'
Telling their children, 'See you soon' when they cried.
But their wives read the bleak truth in their eyes.
As their lifeboats dropped over the side.
The ocean was rushing into the ship.
And hundreds were trapped down below.
The cold had us all in its icy grip.
God knows what it was like in the sea!
It was ten below zero upon the ship.
It felt more like fifteen to me.
The bow was now tilting, the stern was rising,
And most were resigned to their fate,
Everything was sliding, and there was no disguising,
That for us it was already too late.
I remember thinking how bright the stars were,
How they twinkled in that clear dark sky.
I tried not to think of what was going to occur,
'Cause oh I did not want to die . . .
I and others tried to climb up the stern,
Some jumped to their deaths below.
I knew this was the point of no return,
As I watched those in the lifeboats row;
Row as hard as they possibly could,
Or they would be pulled down with Titanic
When she finally sank, as she would.
The band was playing, their courage gigantic,

As they sank with the ship 'neath the sea.
I clung to the stern as it rose in the air.
Then I jumped into that icy black sea.

Oh yes, I sailed on the great Titanic,
And I died with her on that night,
As we sank beneath the Atlantic,
Hidden forever away from the light.
And here I lie 'neath the shifting sand,
Though my soul is forever free.
And I still hear the sound of the band,
Playing on 'til eternity.
And the steerage still echoes with laughter,
And the fiddler still can be heard,
Playing in the 'hereafter',
As he did in the living world.

Betty Buckle

DRESSED FOR QUESTIONS

I never asked so many questions when looking back.
Like why was I wicked in shorts?
Or why was I evil in a sleeveless pullover and flares around the home?
Further down the line; why did I act the way
I looked, wearing a pilot jacket, boots and jeans?
Getting bloody noses didn't really make me think
A while later, was dashing nasty?
Or was nasty dashing?
With a criminal record, I was going mad!
After the bruises and hospital visits,
Why was I wearing a belt that didn't hold my jeans up?
I had taken the attire of a drunk.
Lastly, why was self-control so meagre when I quit the booze?
As I pull on my new Doc Martens.
I come to accept, the clothes and footwear I've worn were always me.
A shit if you'd like!

Thomas Baxter

RAGING STORM

Seven months ago the nightmare began,
For a reason that I don't know!
When chronic insomnia turned my life upside down
Each terrible night the questions and tears would flow.

Like an unexpected tornado it crashed into my life,
This silent destroyer and whirlwind of death,
Its relentless battering soon took its toll,
God please take this away or withhold my next breath.

Despondency, turmoil and confusion take hold,
Sickness and frustration replace my hopes and dreams,
A black hole of despair threatens to swallow me whole,
Another big setback and I rapidly unravel at the seams.

A debilitating condition that if death were to come now,
It would seem like a sweet and tender kiss,
To relieve me from this merciless and unending torture,
Instead I'd sleep forever in God's arms, pure bliss . . .

Overwhelming, stressful, strenuous and left so fragile,
Our whole world has drastically changed,
Consumed by sheer exhaustion feels like mental rape,
The pain's excruciating, like I'm going deranged . . .

Each day is a total blur and merely rolls into the next,
I find myself wandering in a cruel mental maze,
Everything/one/sound and thought
Leaves me in a constant and frazzled daze.

Life's become a major struggle to survive,
'God, will you take this evil tormentor away?'
I feel your reassuring presence close to me,
You're not going to leave me this way . . .

Dawn Madigan

TOGETHERNESS

(Cameron's Curse)

So they dropped the bomb: Armageddon.
Nation's confrontation, met head on.
Swift retaliation: Apocalypse.
The final slip 'twixt cup and lips.

Chain reaction, north, south, east and west,
Mother Nature shows her vicious best
They said it couldn't happen, it's too late,
'Twas man's hand pushed the button: Detonate.

The deed is done. The die is cast,
Lucky ones incinerated by the blast,
Unlucky ones lead horrible short lives,
The end of days, nothing survives.

The ice caps melt, the oceans race,
Tsunamis gathering speed apace,
Unexpected consequence began,
Submerging every last vestige of man.

The Earth, a radiated ball in space,
Devoid of every creed and race,
Polluted seas and atmospheres,
Contaminated: For a thousand years.

But was this part of some eternal plan,
To end man's inhumanity to man?
This golden opportunity, too good for Him to miss,
To punish man's ungodliness, his greed and avarice.

It almost happened once before, Noah and the flood,
He gave us every chance, we never understood,
He gave us some intelligence, promulgating skill,
It wasn't meant for waging war, to maim, destroy and kill.

Religious leaders, politicians, just could not agree,
Failed negotiations, the end of history,
No winners: No seasons: No weather.
Cameron's contribution,
'We're all in this together.'

Jim Storr

SHATTERED DREAM

So dearly longed for,
Yet not to be,
You were an amorphous mass,
Which quit life suddenly.

Your mother's discomfort and pain,
Became a sudden flood,
When your existence ceased,
In a startling rush of blood.

After early weeks of hope,
Divulged to only a few,
Your mother now has to cope,
With the loss of you.

Once a flicker of light,
A presence in her heart,
The unknowingness of your extinction,
Was an unforeseen painful dart.

There's sadness not to know you,
Nor to have seen your face,
But in your grieving mother's heart,
You'll always have a place.

She did not know your gender,
And still inwardly feels the pain,
But when the mourning's over, she hopes
To achieve full motherhood again.

Suzanna Wilson

ODE TO A STAIN

(A Poem In Doric)

Twa' years ago aroon' the Christmas Fair,
Thir' wis a stain spread oot oan the livin' room flair.
Well Ah' tho'cht, an' Ah tho'cht, 'Whit could it be?'
That mark doon below fair baffled me.

Ah' tho'cht it wis egg, or maybe a spit,
Or somethin' bro'cht it in oan somebody's fi't.
It could'a bin some'dy whae'd jist spilt thir' tea.
Ah'm pretty damn sure it could'ny be me.

Well Ah' spoke tae the wife, an' the cooncil as well,
Ah' very near 'phoned Environmental Health.
Bit naebody could say exactly whit wis the cause,
An' Ah'm, noo nearly cimbin' the livin' room wa's.

Ah' bent doon wi' a cloot an' gave it a wipe.
The smell thit came aff it wis well ower ripe.
Ah' scrubbed it, ah' scraped it, an' washed it until,
Ah' took anither look, an' it was bigger still.

Noo that's twae years gone, an' ah'm nane the wiser.
Ah've tried bleach an' Fairy, an' a boattle o' Tiser.
Ah've nearly pilled ev'ry hair oot o' ma heid,
'Cause whitever it is, it's bin a long time deid.

Well ah'm no' gonn'ae worry masel' nae mair aboot it,
Fir the only thing ah've no tried, is tae bend doon an' sook it.
Ah'll jist ignore it, ah'll walk past an' no' stare.
Bit tho' ah' dinnae care, it's still thair', oan the flair.

Ian W Archibald

REJOICE

A summer of rare delights.
Participants reaching for the heights.
Events to thrill and mesmerise,
Drama and spills to tantalise.
A gathering of nations embracing,
Participating and celebrating.
London proudly hosts the Olympics
After the magnificent historic
River Thames Royal Pageant
Catches our breath in its splendour.
Truly respondent.
Indeed a memorable summer of rare delights.
An emotional rollercoaster for many.
Happiness and gratitude expressed fully
For our dear Diamond Queen and Prince Philip,
In whose reign we are privileged to live.
And our heart-felt thanks we give.

Margaret Ann Wheatley

BLUE BELL WOOD

A carpet of blue beneath my feet
Bluebells swaying in the evening breeze
Butterflies dancing from flower to flower
Spreading their pollen as they flutter about
The ripple of the stream
As it flows through the wood
A drop of rain falls from above
Refreshing the bluebells in the wood
Dappled sunshine can be seen
Through the density of the trees
Such a rare and wondrous sight
Gazing at the bluebells
Beneath my feet.

Doreen Cawley

THE VIEW FROM MY WINDOW

Rolling hills
Covered in green,
Walking past
Hikers are seen.

Grazing sheep
Lazily stroll,
In the lush grass
On the steep knoll.

Seeking birds
Find a safe hedge,
For building a nest
On a strong ledge.

Bumblebees flit
From pansy to rose,
As a white kitten
Paws her pink nose.

Butterflies dance
In bright sunlight,
While a young lad
Flies his new kite.

Without these views,
A humdrum life
Would be endured
By husband and wife.

Kathleen White

IN THIS ROOM

I take the blue paper tissue
And unfold each corner;
An unscented flower;
Paper fortune teller.

And from your soap clean skin
I steal an unmade tear;
These white lies – disguised
Like this sterile room,
With man-made heart.

David Coldwell

THE SPITFIRE AND THE WIND

They sat there in their splendour
Twelve Spitfires, survivors of a great endeavour
The day was to remember their 70 years
How the sight of them helped to calm fears
Their grace and pace
Their daily flights to stop a master race
And the wind it blew
The sky was grey and wet, not bright and blue
What would they do?
Would they fly?
Yet we turned out in our droves to see these majestic crates of the sky
Memories of what they represented brought a tear to the eye
At the hands of a few to save the nation they would fly
Veterans there to sign their names for the bravery they showed in a plane
Not for celebratory but to remember their comrades again
And the wind it blew
The sound of an engine, which brought back thoughts of by-gone days
An icon of grace and pace in many ways
A time when the world was at war
Could these men have done more?
And the wind it blew
Even when the day had such a dark sky
Expectations were running high
To see the Spitfire once again in formation fly
The wind got stronger and stronger
Would it last much longer?
Waiting in the cold would be worth it to see them in the air
To remember what they did was why we were there
Then those words that said, 'To risk them flying would not be fair'
The Spitfire would remain on the ground
We would not hear that collective engine sound
Slowly everyone started to depart
Cold and sad at heart
A seventieth anniversary foiled by a wind that blew.

Derek Gaskell

ROARING REPLETE

Heavenward and strong, the sun was golden in its throng,
The angelus plied high and the harps and trumpets blaring
And praying in the wind
That was soulful and endearing;
And time lay down to see the stars
As they shone on the keeps of the shepherds fast asleep,
With the moonstones flaring and the blessed cattle raining
And the heartstrings of Easter
Flashing in the veins.

And knelled among bells in their presidential cells
That scuttered in the skippings like an evening on a hill –
In the wafers and the wines
Of the wynding whorls of time –
God's wishes reared and careered down the stairs
Of Jacob, and nothing could be shattered or constrained,
Nor any world of violence be refrained into the licence
Of the world, as God's children
Bellowed in their joyfulness so deep –

And nobody, not a thing, could sour the Earth of springs
And fallowed in the arbours of the heavens and the skies –
And the mad moon moved
Like a stone upon the water –
And to wake forever and to hear the bells of pleasure
And the coiling curls of wisdom unravelling far away!
O yes when the lord was new to his word
And the flittering apostles siblings in their speech,
Rhyme and her brides lay regal undertides, roaring replete!

Jed Bellamy

AWESOMENESS

The almighty Lord, is an amazing being,
Most beautiful and pure like a diamond ring.
He is closer than you think
In every person and every blink.
Such hands have created this universe,
Within our hearts, deeply immerse.
God's message is clear, our ways need to mend,
To think of all as one's friend
The world around is full of grace,
As we learn to admire this beautiful place.
The key to life is love for all,
And you will hear God's call.

Sukhbinder Kaur

CRUEL

(In memory of Garry Taberer 25/5/2005 Coral Taberer (Rennie's Dad))

Tears fall freely from her eyes, as she looks across the room,
This little girl, 12 years of age, maturity came too soon,
Life so far had been so cruel, and lay heavy on her heart,
Her dad no longer here for her, sadly had to part,
Grief is a funny thing you see,
Because she was only five,
The fading memory of her dad,
Was the last time she'd seen him alive
Seven years later, mixed emotions evidently to see,
This little girl, my daughter, who stands in front of me,
Questions, questions, I'm left to face,
Through one man's act, that has left this space,
In my child's heart, this pain too much to bear,
This terrible thing has happened and it's the reason her dad's not there,
So when she turns her head with that look upon her face,
Hurting, wondering, thinking, whilst her dad's in 'another place,'
She often asks, why my dad, how could this be?
Tears falling, asking, 'Why, why, why did this happen to me?'
I cannot answer her questions, I can only turn to her and say,
I would go to the end of the Earth for you to take your pain away.
I doubt if that will ever happen I know her pain's too deep
So I gently stroke her head and watch her while she sleeps.

Jacqueline Rennie

MIRRORED MEMORIES

I gazed at my reflection in the early morning light
Mind perplexed as I saw the stranger before me
Old age has sailed in on a fast moving breeze
Changing my life with uncomfortable ease
It caught me out when I was least aware
Advancing the years with never a care
With some trepidation and palpating heart
I sit and wait for a new chapter to start
In the darkness every nerve is stripped down bare
Every day is so much longer now my children aren't there
Dare I say out loud that I am lonely and blue
Shall I smile and pretend I am fine without you
I age and I tire, I sleep and I cry
For the days of fulfilment that have passed me by
Silence is often deafening
Peace is not all that it seems
A house filled with laughter is now only in my dreams
These days I wake up with a creak and a groan
Life seems to hold many reasons to moan
We all struggle to understand the shadows of life
How we lose individuality to be a mother and a wife
Volumes of knowledge sit behind my aged eyes
They speak of a time I thought I was wise
Do not dismiss my presence or think I am done
For within this ageing body there is still lots of fun
Strength is needed to create your own fate
There is only nonsense in anger and hate
I will open my arms and embrace each brand new day
For this is no rehearsal just a means to pave the way
Life is short, the ending untold
At the end of the rainbow there is no pot of gold
There are simply the smiles that make every day
And the wonderful words our children say
Rise up and sing, give thanks for every breath
For you cannot be certain how many days are left.

Lynn Noone

BUTTERFLIES GO SERENDIPITY

Butterflies flit along serendipity!
They are so light
That human things such as worry or care
Just couldn't sit upon their wings . . .
First they are here
Then they are there
They're so very flittery
That you simply do not realise how
Much space they cover
Until you really, really watch . . .
Forming dapples here, dapples there
They're so elegant in their simplicity
Because butterflies go serendipity!

Susan Fenelon

THE STORY OF MY LIFE

The years are flying by
Recalling a yesterday
Under white fleecy clouds
In a powder-blue sky.

Watching a busy bee fly by
Over the clover leaf flowers
Sipping the honey
Washed by early showers.

The message is clear
A bumblebee's flight
To watch in delight
To be lonely is a figure of speech.

Like the bee it only needs to reach
The beauty of love and happiness
Free for the taking in Nature's store
And never be alone.

Joan Hands

HYPOCRISY/ARISTOCRACY

Very seldom do we refer to want and need;
As pure and simple aristocratic greed.
Disheartening tricks learned from the top;
Now a wielding axe ready for the chop.
Dressage of the Royal Mint, for so long seemed to go well;
But at the last fence, the monetary horse, it fell.
And now the anger is out there, it's on the hunt for meat;
Searching the private boy's clubs and the penthouse suite.
It wasn't my fault, so it must have been yours.
Gallant games played by penny pounding whores.
Point at you with our arrows of blame;
Designed to adjust the focus, designed to maim.
I do not gamble with money, I do as I am told;
I merely sign the dotted line for the things I am sold.
New clothes, shoes and gifts of flowers;
Losing their appeal with the passing of hours.
And so we keep on spending, keep the wardrobes turning.
Forgetting that really it's our money we're burning.
We may not have company credit cards or sit behind desks with screens;
But we ought to be at least clear of what this means.
Perhaps we can't take the blame, but maybe it's a burden to be shared.
The truth of the matter is nobody cared.
Set in our panic, frustration starting to encase
Realising the responsibility we now have to face.

Ethan R Chapples

USE YOUR MIND LIKE A CHAMPION!

Use your mind like a champion!
When the rains move upon the moonshine
The hour will ask, 'What will be mine?'
The Champion that won asked no question indeed!
It gave way to move swiftly up to succeed.

Use your mind like a Champion!

Caroline Champion

MY HERO 1805

Lord Nelson nearly lost that war,
He hadn't many frigates,
And those bigots at the Admiralty
short-changed on rum and salted nuts.
The sailors did their best, of course
on hard tack and bitter beer,
But Nelson must have liked a tot
because he sailed to Whitehall Pier.
He strolled around Saint James's Park
to ponder on his plight,
And while he fed the pelicans,
the answer came to light.

It's there, he cried, the House of Lords,
I'm out at sea so much,
I must pop in and plead my case,
They are really out of touch!
Next day, the House was full of Peers,
Lord Nelson took his seat,
Debate went on and on and on,
They screamed and stamped their feet,
Till Nelson rose and winked his eye,
He was certain his time had come,
How, he said, to those men so rich
can we find peace without ships or rum?

If you put more into the pot
I'll squash those Frogs and Dons I swear!
So give Great Britain all you've got
and show the people that you care!
Cheers all round, the pot overflowed,
What did they get, History will say
he sank the naughty Frogs and Dons
but, sadly lost his life that day.
So if you visit Charing Cross,
Look ever so high in the air,
You should see my hero standing
on his column in Trafalgar Square.

Alan Smith

THE OLD SEA CHEST

I inherited an old house,
Where my Auntie Winn and Uncle Jack used to live,
With it's Victorian furniture and antiques within.

In the attic upstairs, memorabilia stored,
An old sea chest caught my eye.

With initials A. R. inscribed in gold letters,
A captain's hat and uniform,
A photograph of him and his wife,
Lay inside.

Underneath, kept in a carved ivory box,
A lock of hair encased in a locket.
And letters tied with blue ribbon.

His name was Alan Ramsey,
Captain of the Marianne
Named after his wife.

Lynda Sergent

9/11

Their tears of love will always flow
Their tears of love
Their tears of love
For they have nowhere else to go
Their tears of love
Their tears of love
So much pain so many tears of loved ones lost
Ten million mothers' tears shall flow
A waterfall of love
Their tears have nowhere else to go
Have faith they are not lost
But maybe just maybe their love for us
In our hearts will grow
And maybe just maybe their love for us
In our hearts will grow
And maybe just maybe the tears that
Touch our face
Are their kisses to let us know.

Nicky Anderson

PERFECT AS A FLOWER

Jesus, thank you for this minute
How wonderful to see
The flowers as they bend
In the wind

They are beautiful to see
Look at them – their faces
Shining bright.

With petals that glow
In their colours of light
As you look at the flowers.

Let your heart know
The Creator made them
So that you would know
That His love for you
Is forever true.

Perfect as a flower
Is His love for you.

Val Backs

HIGH TEA AT HENLEY-ON-THAMES 1947-1999

Many teas for two were shared at Henley-on-Thames
With my Aunt Elsie tea with my aunt
At Henley in 1959 and in 1963
Many teas with Elsie at Henley
An aunt I adored and continue to applaud
There were many more from the age of eight
Till 1999 (when she died) teas with the family
Hers and mine on a Sunday visit at three
At Henley with Auntie Elsie
Our teas for two however were between her and me
Her niece, daughter of Dorothy from London
Dorothy a trail-blazer supreme during the 1930s
And me on holidays to Henley at weekends
Via train from Paddington Green
She in her kitchen busy and organised
Ensuring all was ready and correct for tea
And me at the dining table waiting and listening
Intently bread and butter jam sultana
Scones and cream strawberries as a treat
Tea for two with my Aunt Elsie pleased as punch
Thrilled to my knees to be taking tea
With dear Elsie a chum and so very generous
Always to me at Henley out and away on a spree.

Margaret Bennett

HER OLD SELF

The worst is over, she's on the mend
Quite her old self again, mourning must end.
It hurts like hell, we know that's true
You're not alone, we've been there too.

The day will come, it will, you'll see,
When sorrow lifts and sets you free
Think of others, think of him
What good is life when the lights go dim?

Why linger on when it's time to go?
Life moves on, like the rivers flow.
He's out of pain now, it's better so,
It's crueller far when death comes slow.

Your time will come, we all must go,
He'll wait for you, be it fast or slow.
Don't be selfish. The kids need you,
And there's so very much to do.

Find support groups. Talk to Cruse
Contact Dateline. What's to lose?
So much to give, you mustn't mope
We'd miss you so, there's always hope.

When one door shuts . . . It's a bitter blow,
But the world's your oyster – on you go.
You'll love again, the world is wide,
You're much too young to run and hide.

Talk to friends, you mustn't brood.
(Don't bother Mum, she's in a mood)
Work for others, make new friends.
God needs you to shape his ends.

We knew you'd cope, we told you so
Time heals all – *But what do they know!*

Dory Phillips

TIGER LADY (LOOKING FOR SOME SERIOUS FUN)

Trapped no longer
Released from captivity.

Soft kissable lips
Tease to please.

Sexual body signals
Serious fun intended.

Wild flowing hair
Tamed hungry look.

Seductive pleasure curves
Purring with desire.

Smiling eyes transfix
Passionate magical trance.

Scented to arouse
Honey trap set.

Breaking the ice
Casual relaxed conversation.

Laughing and joking
Close friendship discovered.

Two strangers disappear
Intimacy grows strong.

Samantha quietly says
Today is special

Birth certificate states
I am male.

This is my
First time out.

OK Tiger Lady
Midnight supper waits.

Tonight is ours
Till love surrenders.

Nigel Astell

THE MOCKING BIRD

Are you one who has danced with the Devil by chance or by choice
Are you quick to obey all the orders of each Master's voice
Repeating the lives of our Fathers while blinded by faith
Expectant of love and forgiveness for life's mistakes we make.

We live in a time where the blind are still leading the strong
Are the righteous self-righteous enough to be righteously wrong
Excuse is the 'crutch' that we're human, exempt from perfection
Will that be the cross that we bear when we're faced with rejection

Are those passing before us the wiser for passing at all
Are the heights that we reach for in life our reasons to fall
Is there peace of the mind or the spirit in Heaven or Hell
Does sin linger eternally damning . . . a putrescent smell

Does the human within us insist that we make life's mistakes
As we wrestle our conscience, the innocent life in our wake
Should we wish for forgiveness or wallow . . . only time will tell
When it's too late for unanswered questions . . . will the mocking bird yell

What is left as humanity waits on the last curtain call
Will we rise to the Heavens above as the last angels fall
Will our wonder be wonder alone that the Heavens replace
Shall we plunge to the depths of despair even further from grace

Does time fly on wings that will heal the broken and damned
Will faith be the cure for the festering wounds in his hands
No redemption for those admitting we're wrong and afraid
Destroying the beauty around us in the nightmares we've made.

Lord help us repent now we're dreadfully lost and alone
No chance for to change does our future lie written in stone
Can we change who we are, can we change that which tears us apart
Are we wasting our time are the children alone pure of heart

Was Jesus shown human while losing his temper . . . seems odd
Is it sinful to think that we're made in the likeness of God
Is each personal quest less important, less noble to call
Then those that lay prone at the foot of the Wailing Wall
You decide for yourselves . . . but for me
I don't think so . . . at all!

Peter Walsh

THOSE NORTHERN HILLS

With spring approaching and winter fading fast
I look to the northern hills
To get some peace at last
Rucksack at the ready, fill my tank with juice
Five hours up the motorway finally cutting loose
Untie the knot and full sail on the mast
A steady wind behind me blows away the past
In all my years of driving up that motorway
It's never been harder than it is today
Even a drawn departure doesn't help at all
There always seems to be a solid moving wall
Maybe after midnight you have a fighting chance
Downing cans of Red Bull does seem to enhance
Sharper concentration, now I want to dance
Winding my way through Langdale in the early morning light
Green hills, like walls surround me
There is no finer sight
Except a pint of Catnap at the Sticklebarn
Poured by a pretty barmaid with tattoos on her arm
Although the spring's approaching there is a snow alert
Alas upon arrival the weather is inert
It has passed me by I fear
It's headed south to Bedfordshire.

Philip Hutson

DECAYING SKIN

I want to be dust
Floating in the carefree air
Free to roam on breathless sighs
Empty, yet consumed
I want to be skinless
Shoulder blades etching like swans
From my decomposing back
So beautifully created
Under my delicate decaying mask
Painting red skies onto my skin
The pain-staking sky washes over me
Brushing through my pores
And leaving trails of crimson secrets
That my lips daren't ever tell
Deliverance, decadence, fragility
A breath-taking numbness
Cold to the touch, and lifeless to the bone
My frayed mentality, forever wearing away
With each battered and weathered memory
Etching themselves onto my brain
Like an artist's masterpiece
That encompasses his soul
Forever waiting . . . just waiting
For that masterpiece to be understood
As beauty, and not a delicate mess.

Anne-Marie Large

THE INTELLIGENT MAN

'Don't mix up the colours, keep them where they are!'
'Separate the grains of sand from each and every jar!'
'Wash your hands again, don't leave clothes on the floor!'
'I don't want to hear it, you're not opening that door!'
'Please organise the shoes in size order, smallest to the left;
Don't seek a compromise what's normal is always best!'
'Shave the hairs off your head in a perfectly straight line!'
'Washing them is so much effort, I simply don't have time!'
Sorry for that outburst, I was just having my way.
Whenever people make a mistake, I cannot help but say.
To put it simply, keeping things in order makes my pain go away.
I like to have things neat and tidy, fresh and new;
Don't try to make a mess, or I might have to correct you.
When I was younger, no one understood my dream;
To make the world and myself perfectly clean, I would often
Pick flower petals so they were an even digit; when my
Schoolmates had mud fights; I would stand there and fidget.
My teacher said to me once, 'What is the matter with you?'
And I simply replied, 'You wouldn't have a clue;
Everything I see is full of imperfections, cars driving in the wrong directions,
And people's crooked eyes showing painful reflections.'
She really didn't know what to say, she referred me to a doctor
The next day; he tried hypnosis, medication, therapy and isolation.
But the only thing that came of it was an official declaration;
I have obsessive-compulsive disorder, so I suppose I have been branded;
I don't know what it really is, but sometimes I feel stranded.
My parents still look after me in their old age;
You've got to love them for that, because everyone else thinks I'm strange.

Isaac Lewis

MUTED SHYNESS

A failure's frown and a sunken smile
Written across my face
My uncomfortable eyes and suspicious looks
Darting all around

I try to hide these tremor ridden hands
And tapping feet
My racing heart and shallow breath
Are easier to disguise

Contradicting mind, thoughts accelerate
Yet no words make a sound,
Just an outer shell muted by this curse
An extravert inside of me
Which doesn't allow the world to see

Judgemental feelings, am I weak?
Every thought to speak overwhelms me,
Each sentence and word combine
They mix and form to one
A senseless mould of comprehension
Which appears and then it's gone

Fear of embarrassment and rejection is now a rule
A belief imprinted in my soul
Looked upon with fear, aggression or pity

It's holding him back I hear them say
Believing I am not seen as I am not heard
Furious that they say these things
It only makes it worse.

David Bull

TANGENTS

Viewing life from angles
May prove confusing task
Kiddies clutching spangles
May hit the streets and gasp

Chance of being furthered
Advanced in life's rich game
May prove so vaguely worded
When not recognised the same

It's meeting life's agenda
Of what to say and how
Knowing how to send her
As children learn to bow

All thinking's seen distorted
If beaten in the street
With all ambition thwarted
As violent tangents meet.

Tracy Allott

ACHIEVING EVERYTHING

Falling deeply into my own silence
Falling deeply in tune with timeless silence
In that silent harmony
All is achieved

This is the art of finding my way home
In that silent innocence
Is openness and receptivity
And my being begins to resonate
With that which has always been

And in that resonance I realise
That I have never really lost my way
I had just forgotten
That this is my home.

William Weavings

DELIGHTFULLY DELUDED

Standing on the edge of insanity
Trapped by my own mental delusions
Shackled down by oppression

Unable to escape my reality

It has become hard
To differentiate between reality
And my own fantasies

I'm left in a confusional state

With no orientation . . .
To time, place or person
My delusions getting the better of me

Paranoia is all that defines me

I have to escape from this psychosis
But it's like they're all watching me
Got me watching my back

I'm on edge continuously . . .

The whispers getting ever so loud
I'm preoccupied with my own hallucinations

Disconnected from the realms of humanity
It's like I died . . .

. . . and I'm only here spiritually

Cos how can I tell if I'm alive?
When there is no certainty
Cos there is a difference
Between living . . . and just being alive

But . . . it's all grey to me

I need some sort of illusion
To get me away from all this negativity
Cos the edge is about to crumble

And I fear what's down below me . . .

But it turns out,
Reality is just a dream
Cos we're on a really long journey

Where nothing is as it seems . . .

Our final destination
Seeming a lifetime away

. . . We get deceived

So maybe my insanity
Is a way of saving me

And being riddled with delusions . . .
Is how I'll finally be set free

Cos these delusions are my escape
From the man-made shackles

. . . Geared towards you and me

Got everyone riding the waves of oppression
Till they can no longer see

It's like they're deaf, dumb and blind
Moving further into darkness . . .

. . . Unhinged for eternity . . .

I prefer my delusions . . .

. . . Do you blame me?

Sally Babiker

OUR WORLD

Have you seen the sky at night
The distant stars all shining bright?
Have you stood and looked in awe
At all the wonders and much more?

Have you seen a springtime dream
Where trees stand tall in newborn green?
Flowers peep from behind the earth
And all of Mother Nature awaits rebirth.

Summer sun and drowsy bees
A profusion of flowers in copse and lea
Flamboyant colours and falling leaves
Golden days their warmth near spent
The last rose of summer head now bent

Now glimpse a winter wonderland
Trees dressed in white so proud and grand
Sparkling frost and cold sharp air
Your world and mine to love and share.

Sylvia Partridge

A LONG DARK TUNNEL (A CANCER PATIENT'S JOURNEY)

I entered a long dark tunnel feeling lonely and afraid.
I reached inside for courage my confidence betrayed.
The darkness overwhelmed me, stripped me naked of all hope,
I must recover dignity and find a way to cope.
Each step a test of character I struggled with my fear.
Wondering in desperation for my insecurity to clear.
I stood alone and closed my eyes
Breathing deeply I realised,
To fight these demons in my mind
It's me who I must really find.
And of all the emotions I've been through
Love is the one that's been steadfast and true.
The tunnel seemed less daunting as I went along my way,
Did my treatment work at last?
Will I see the light of day?
'Look my wife has made it through,'
And in our hearts we always knew,
Her determination and love for life,
Has turned her darkness into light.

James Walls

SCHOOL DAYS

Memories forever in mind
Holding on to a lost time
The days we had so fun and free
Those days again I'd like to see
Walking in the sun, walking in the rain
School is a place we can never go again
Those days are over those days are gone
Time to look to the future and carry on.

Sadie Shaw

UNTITLED

With a glimmering hope, but –
Also with fear of recognition
You survey the vast perimeters;
Searching – for the lustful man of copper;
And the adulterated henna in his blazing eyes.
You know you must see the wild man,
To beat the cracking ice in your knuckles –
To mute the hot steam pouring from –
The memories; of you two making beasts with two backs.
You must see the creature of the horizon
And dance with him tonight;
Dance on the horizon, of –
On the horizon of your wounded rubble of a soul.
You must feel once more the sinking of;
The bowels within your frame, and;
The air he breathes out; enter you just once more.
Nobody knows you are here, standing –
At the barrel of a gun; laid out in;
Henna, at the risk of your own –
Sanity pulling the trigger.
He always comes at the time of –
Hesitation before your birth.
You wove a lie out of an obnoxious obsession,
A treacherous and; rotten love –
That penetrates its rusty fingers; to the core.
It is a lie of a life not lived –
A promise, never realised;
A century of bitter punishment; and guilt.

Tatiana Aksarova

BREATH OF THE ENCHANTED CHILD

You are my high
So I will fly
Close to your light,
Knowing full well
That my heart will melt

You are mercy,
A cool breeze
On a blistering day
I find my lost self
In your laughter

You are my night
I watch you sleep,
Chest rise and fall
In angel time
Breath of the enchanted child
Blesses your face

You are my teacher,
Why do you trust in me?
I am not so good
Or wise or kind
Or worthy.

You are my life.
In each heartbeat
You live in me
Breaking me down
With starlight tears

You are my night
I watch you sleep,
Chest rise and fall,
In angel time
Breath of the enchanted child
Blesses your face.

Beth Ditson

ACCEPTANCE

I accept that you are you
And that I am me

I accept that we breathe to live
And in the end we die

I accept the consequences that follow on from the choices we make

I have the choice of getting anything I want
But I know the consequences could mean losing everything

I accept that it will never always be buy one get one free on all essentials
And I guess I'll have to accept that I will have to give up on some luxuries

I know one day I will chose the completely wrong outfit
But, I'm just going to have to accept that, I may just look hideous

I will accept I am a nice person
I will accept I can be a bad person . . . sometimes

I accept times will be tough
I choose to hide my feelings and the pain
I understand that this may push loved ones away

I also accept that there will be times when I will be utterly alone
And that there will be times where I will be surrounded by friends and family in one, massive, loving hoard

I also understand I will be hurt more times than I already have
I know that I'm going to be lied to, and just maybe, I won't find the truth

I accept life will start out as though God is out to get me
But, I also understand that the end of this life will be beautiful and peaceful

I have chosen to get married and to be with this person until death do us part
And I accept that the consequence means never being with my sweetheart

I appreciate the fact that this life is short
I also accept that this world is changing
And that one day it will all disappear

I also know that one day; I will bring a life into this world
I know they will experience everything I have, will, and maybe more
I understand that the consequence of bringing life into this world means that they will die too

This doesn't make me selfish; we all make choices and in the end, we just need to accept our mistakes.

Emma Croshaw

THE BARD BLEEDS

An imaginary box,
Harnessed by muted fury.
A carousel.
Silhouettes of family and friends.
Idle contemplation.
A broken record; bemusing musical virtuosos by sheer novelty and spectacle.
Perceived reality.
Psychiatrists all over the nation brandish their filo-faxes.

Posthumous applause.

Jaxx King

SOWING THE SEEDS

Hatred, anger, I once was a child,
Love, happiness I never knew,
So cruel, I cannot hate
Who is locking my happiness away?
Was it him? I think it was
Preying on my vulnerability
I never felt love like that
So special, yet so stupid.

I now have sown my own seeds
Seeds of hope and love
I need them to grow into beauty
Make my love grow into good things
No more tears, no more fights,
Bye-bye pressure, a weight lifted
Flowers started growing again
Happiness is coming again.

Angela Connors

DAMAGED

Thoughts hang on unanswered questions
Memories burn on flames of fear,
Pain and hurt are best companions
Where love and compassion just disappear.
Regret is something that scars me deeply
Wounds my soul and plagues my mind,
Silent words are left unspoken
By selfish people who are far too blind.
Stubbornness builds a wall
Brick by brick a prison cell,
And hate seeps like a poison
Where no one seems to break the spell.
A victim of my own kindness
That's bled me to a sorry state,
Black and white the person I am
Seeing true colour came too late.
Damaged am I by life and people
Who used and abused me
Yet saw no shame,
I point not one finger
For I only have myself to blame.
To hurt an angel who's loving and giving
Here to walk and shed their light,
To wound and break their gentle wings
Takes away their immortal right,
And with this comes a heavy sentence
The feel of pain and a broken heart,
Blood that runs from scars wide open
A soul completely ripped apart.
Damaged am I by life and people
Who used and abused me
Yet saw no shame,
For I point not one finger
I only have myself to blame.
Not seeing these people
For who they were
Underneath their selfish ways,
But I know God will pay them back
Counting down their numbered days.

Lisa Mills

SINNER'S HOPE

There was a touch,
That found its fuel,
There wasn't much,
But it found you

. . . and all the times I'd given up
And all the limitations of love
All the bargains I had made
You had blown them all away

And in came passion, in came fear
And I was getting out of there
I've thought a lot, I've wasted time
But I never thought that you'd be mine

If pride's a sin, I'm far gone
But I'm coming up, I'm not alone
Wrath is mine, and envy too
But so is hope, and it's from you

I know that we're all mortal
And life can cloud the eyes
If you crawl, I'll help you walk
And your problems will be mine

You're my sense of beauty
And I'll always be in your debt
I'm around till you don't want me
Because my dear, it ain't forever yet

I'll speak of love without shame
And I will find joy anew
I'm alive again and you're to blame
Hannah, this one goes out to you.

Philip Richards

VOICE OF OUR CHILDREN

Take heed without question for change has been born
New philosophies to digest from every lesson and reform
Harsh is the truth that haunts thee through time
Punishments unholy, no sanctity in our crime
Bloodshed so frequent masterminded through greed
Reverence unworthy, apocalyptic without need
Dominant of the masses deliriously insane
Predatory without conscience, no honour to claim
Outrageous resistance no fight left for war
Only slaughtered bloody civilians who cry out no more
Listen to the ghosts, as they wail for man's sins
Muffled deathly silence, life without meaning
Holocaustic proportions, a world's epic to destroy
Mankind's quest for harmony turned hegemony, as we die
Agonies all so obvious, as the poor always pay
Bodies lost in rubble, their bones left to decay
Still we dream of horizons innocent and pure
An antidote for living a miracle and a cure
May the children of tomorrow give what we've lost
Their voice our salvation, yet cursed by the cost.

Lee Hunt

STRIKE, STRIKE, STRIKE

There has been a big walkout at work,
We are all over-worked and under-paid.
Office closures and redundancies are a threat,
Unfortunately meaning job losses,
So the union took the democratic decision,
To strike, strike, strike,
Hoping for the bosses to listen,
For three whole days,
We won't get paid.
Our solidarity is our strength,
So please don't stamp out our service,
As we don't deserve it!

Tina Rooney

CARRIERS AND HARRIERS

Carriers and harriers
Synonymous I would say
Cameron couldn't see it
And gave them all away

Now Kempston Secondary Modern
With Eaton can't compare
But my simple education
I think was very fair

I'm not well versed in the arts
Or ideas of Genteel Design
But in defence of my country
I knew how to stand in line

And while that there's a Britain
Where the British should be free
Where there's the choice of freedom
And the rule of democracy

We need a better leader
The question who is he
The deaf cannot hear
And the blind cannot see

If I make so bold sir
In the cause of liberty
Only one man springs to mind?
Nigel Farage is the name

If you want an independent Britain
Place your vote beside his name.

Brian Vissian

A LEGENDARY DANGEROUS WAY

Legarious ways, when cut of choice was spent
on useless veins of flesh and simple thoughts
A cure was always there as I permitted sin,
while stale and wasted, sat in squalor,
screamed for needle's hit, within a crazy mind,
along gaping gutters, those dregs that were a life.

Would you ever, in such eyes as these, have sockets sold?
Skeletal hung like dripping paint upon a blistered door,
hinged wafer thin, discoloured death paste, passing
upon streets so cold for penetrating fingertips,
all primed to detonate the very living soul in me.

Then I recalled conversations from a different world,
where laughter wasn't scorn, but jollied warmer times.
It spoke of children and the meadow fields of old,
folded letters and some photographs of fresher ways,
expressed a scene, of innocence, a fleshy gait of
uncomplicated strut, setting confidence alight to burn.

What of the head that rolled straight off that doll?
Giving place to troubled ways and hollowed bones,
bleeding dreams into nightmares' bended ways,
conducting courtships dark, setting soul ablaze.

Belong to fashions of addiction, a price is paid,
laying here this wasted shell, hearing words
of trip and fall pity, I didn't dare listen!
Can you hear the hopeless fading of another call?
The hopscotch games of childhood play on chalks,
were lines formed deep, lonely passage walks
so soiled, of my abandoned city ways, for sure.

Away from those, who dismissed a closer look,
as cobbled life was set in concrete shoes, on feet
unstable for any acquiescent weekly strolls.
An innocent bystander caught in the expectations
many placed upon the shoulders of a gifted child.

Now mind-chains strangling shackles are undone,
flown, way above the heads from where you stand,
What a blame? Go dry your eyes to see some peace,
and know from here, a dark entombed farewell.
It was nothing that you did or nothing that you said,
for a cure was always there, but I permitted sin instead.

Michael Bracken

ABATTOIR LOVE

A Firelighter and Snow are on a date,
The cocktails flow, the hour late,
Playing it cool and dancing with fire,
The couple fuse on an Arctic Pyre.

As opposite as Heaven and Hell,
It's a pity they don't heed the warning bell,
A spark of attraction with either slay,
Like Holmes and Moriarity on the cliff that day.

Napoleon and Wellington in a Scorpion waltz,
Their fears vibrate like crystal quartz,
No middle ground can ere be found,
Consummation will end in the burial mound.

When days are dark and nights are long,
And your memories ignited by that 'Special Song',
Remember the millions of the Human Fleet,
Who don't know what it is to be turned, from Snow to Sleet.

Edward Daly

THE PET DOG

There was a young woman from Tassa
Who owned a quiet friendly pet dog.
While on her travels through Carrive
On a fine January evening in 2012.
It got out of control when it saw sheep.
It followed the sheep and killed one.
She shouted stop, but it paid no heed.
It viciously attacked another sheep.
The owner of the sheep followed it with his jeep.
Hitting it in the front leg accidentally.
It was able to run away and went missing.
After a fortnight it appeared home.
Such a sorrowful sight.
Its leg had to be amputated.
Her pet dog is now in good health.
And has learned a very sore lesson.

Michael McGuigan

THE DREAM

When I strolled down to the farm
They said to expect a surprise
And when I saw the animals
I couldn't believe my eyes.

Familiar cows had now turned green
Horses a deep shade of blue
But when I saw the lavender chicks
My astonishment grew and grew.

'What's going on?' I started to say
But there was nobody there
Then a purple donkey passed me by
And gave me a puzzled stare.

'You've still got time to change,' he said
'The show doesn't start for an hour
The changing rooms are just down there
If I were you, I'd have a shower.'

Well, I thought, *what a thing to say*
What was it that he implied
But still I went to the changing rooms
When I saw the mess, I just sat and cried.

Straw and grass lay everywhere
Tins of paint, some of them new
The lavender chicks started running away
'Oh dear,' I cried, 'what shall I do?'

It was then that I awoke
And saw it was just a dream
That was when I knew for sure
Things aren't always what they seem

I hope one day I'll go back again
It really was a wonderful sight
And the lavender chicks will all return
One day perhaps, they all just might.

Barry Winters

TOUSLED SHEETS

In the cool
Of a plentiful night,
An owl calling
Through the trees
A zephyr breeze
Rustling a curtain's shadow,
He climbed the ivy spider-covered walls,
To be with her,
In tousled sheets,
And tousled them some more
In the heat
Of a crimson dawn.

Leigh Jones

GRANDAD

I remember sitting on your lap,
Years ago,
And seeing your face smiling down at me.
I remember our trip on a boat
Down to Greenwich.
I remember your eyes in the hospital,
Turned yellowish, but still crinkled in the corners as you smiled.
I remember the bag, hung discretely under the bedclothes because you couldn't get up.
Mum told me not to ask questions.
I remember sitting on your bed as you lay there,
I thought the ward smelt funny.
I remember trying to memorise the shape of your nose on that last visit.
I remember asking God to give you a message,
Because I couldn't tell you myself.

Every day since then,
I'll remember.

Naomi Abrams

CLIMATE CHANGE

Raindrops batter against our windowpanes
As gusts of wind rattle our doors, our summer
Seems to be changing into autumn or winter
With just a dash of sunshine. A cocktail
Of different weather fronts all in one go
Dull dark days in the middle of June.

We have one or two sunshine days if we are lucky.
Too cold for swimming costumes for children
To play in paddling pools in the garden,
On holiday we sit shivering by the sea, braving
The elements. Hoping for the clouds to depart
To let the sunlight shine through, it's the middle
Of June.

Heating is on through the day, no cooling fans
Are needed, we're all wrapped up in woollens
And cardigans. Ice cream sales are down
It's soup and a roll in cafés. The British bulldog
Spirit won't let us give way, we still surely
Say the sun will break out today it's the middle
Of June.

Is it goodbye to the lovely summers of yesteryear?
When the men wore hankies over their heads
On the beach trouser legs rolled up to their knees.
The women contentedly sitting in deckchairs wearing
Sundresses, watching the children play with
Bucket and spade. When we had some good
Fun days beside the sea, in the middle of June.

Janet Middleton

FEET

Sid Sen T Pede lived in the garden there
With never in the world a care,
So happy and well, right 'in the pink'
And never once of love did think.

He looked upon his home with pride
Thought not so high, nor very wide,
But as he said, 'You all can see
It's big enough, there's only me.'

Then one day, following his nose,
Tiptoeing on his hundred toes,
He fell in love, which made him figure,
He really needed something bigger.

Somewhere with a swimming pool
To help him keep his ardour cool
Tucked away, with trees behind
(Of the floral perfumed kind).

He hoped his love would be the kind
Willing to leave her ma behind;
He didn't think it very 'cool'
For Ma-in-Law to share his pool.

And though his home was now much bigger,
His future ma had a very large figure
That, with her extra million toes
Would soon 'out of joint' put his nose.

'Oh Millie dear, come marry me,'
Said Sid, 'and then you'll see
That in this world so big and wide
No centipede will have more pride.'

'Well,' Millie said, 'I'll have to think;
Can we have our bedroom pink?
And just to prove you really care,
Can I bring all my slippers there?

Well, Sid in love was feeling kind;
'Of course, don't leave all those behind
And bring those boots for when it's cool
And 'Jellies' for the swimming pool.'

Now, though Sid's house was so much bigger
He hadn't really stopped to figure
What the smell, of an extra million toes
Would do to this long suffering nose.

'Millie Pede' he said, 'now hark to me,
I think it's very plain to see,
Your love of shoes is far too wide
You'll have to learn to curb your pride.

I love you yes, but don't you think
A million pairs of boots in pink
Are just too much, or don't you care
That there's no room for me left there?'

Well Millie Pede was not unkind
And didn't want to leave behind
Her Sid, who really was quite 'cool'
(Or do without that swimming pool).

So, though she'd like the cupboards bigger
She thought that, with her swelling figure,
(From the expected billion toes)
For now she'd best 'keep clean' her nose

And so she said to Sid, 'Ah me;
The sense of what you say I see;
I'm growing now so very wide
That though the end will give you pride

It's really best I stop and think,
Of all the future booties pink,
Or blue ones, I don't really care,
But space will sure be needed there.

Now Sid was not the family kind
And thoughts of all he'd left behind,
His little home so nice and cool,
(Much better than that big wet pool)

And in this house, though so much bigger
He felt so cramped; why, he didn't quite figure,
But, crowded with several more million toes!
Well! Just the thought of it got up his nose!

'There'll really be no room for me!
My future's bleak, it's clear to see!
I'm giving up this land so wide,
For peace and comfort; blow the pride!

And Millie-Pede and Ma, I think,
Will likely paint the whole house pink!
To be quite honest, I don't care,
Cos I just won't be living there.'

So, off he went, right then and there

And tootled off without a care,
Though sometimes, something coloured pink,
Might make him pause a while and think.

Did he miss Millie? Did he feel pride
In all his progeny far and wide?
If he a pink dressed Pede did see,
Did he think, *she looks just like me!*

Or did he turn up his smell free nose,
Sniff and say, 'far too many toes.'
Now you are wondering this I figure;
Did Millie Pede's family get any bigger?

Well, last I heard, she owned a pool,
Of typists, who are quick and cool
(With toes in rows, front and behind)
At typing things of every kind.

Gwendoline Lewis

TIMELESS LOVE . . .

T hink of me with timeless love within thy heart as I shall whenever I think of thee.
I n truth, days spent with you are as nectar to the bees sweet, always so sweet . . .
M y love, I miss you more than words could ever say deep within my heart you stay.
E ach and every memory so sublime none shall fade, even with the passage of time . . .
L ove came in so many ways throughout our seemingly carefree halcyon days . . .
E ach time I feel the warmth of sun upon my face and think of you, my heart races.
S weet memories so sublime come flooding back when your lips first kissed mine . . .
S uddenly I feel the warmth of your hand once again gently caressing my own . . .

L onging, always within my heart that you feel the same? Then my wishes come true.
O nly when your eyes meet mine then solace betwixt us comes two hearts beating as one.
V erily the time draws near when feelings run deep and we might shed a tear together.
E mbrace then while we can, the timeless love felt at first, when your eyes met mine.

Michael Counter

WHAT TIME IS

Time is a word
Invented by men
Who invented candles,
Sun dials and clocks,
To measure our stay
In time.

Time is measured yet –
Measureless.
Time is the space between –
The sky and
The Earth
Through which we free-fall or
Deploy our canopies –
For a longer journey.

Time is a granite rock
One hundred miles high
Worn down to a stump
By a sparrow
Which sharpens its beak once –
Every thousand years,
Thus measuring
One day of eternity.

Peter Cranswick

MEDITATIONS OF A LIGHTHOUSE

I rank among the truly great. My boast:
Never succumb to drooping or dejection.
Larger than life I stand, full firm. The most
Magnificent erection.

I see myself protruding with fierce zeal,
Guarding the country's coast so wild and rocky.
Honoured by every man alive, I feel
Indomitably cocky.

I have the wettest dreams you could conceive.
The sea caresses me – and she's a smasher!
Proudly from prehistoric crags I heave –
A seven-second flasher.

Jean Hayes

JUST CAN'T GET ENOUGH

'Wait 'til I get my money right'
Easy to say when you're getting paid at night.
To simply say what I wish I could
If I wouldn't get fired you know I would.
Always in trouble for speaking my mind
I say, 'Yeah right, get with the times.'
You disrespect me and you get it back
No more kissing ass or chasing tracks.
I ain't angry, just saying it as it is
You try and you try, they lie and they lie
'It's just the way it is.'
OK so now is my time
'People say you are wise
Is it because you're a Gemini?'
I say, 'No way! I don't hold my head that high'
But a Gemini like I have two sides
That one you see when you see me
And the nine to five just staying alive.
I can reap the benefits of being good
I can help those who are misunderstood
So I choose to lose all heirs and grace
By being down or wherever that place
Is that you come from I don't always know why
But I relate to that place and eat humble pie.
For we can't stand people who are always right
And we can't bear the thought of harmful homes at night
So we choose to lose and share our woes
Because sadly life isn't ribbons and bows.
A problem shared is a problem halved
'Don't talk shite! Don't even start!'
I can see you be hurting and are in heaps of pain
Come on let's talk, let's start again.
To let go of your anger only sets you free
Your eyes open up and there's nothing you don't see.
I haven't spoken for such a long time
You see I've been busy writing rhymes about life
I'm no longer filling shoes
It's more like I'm feeling you
Feeling you and you're feeling me
It's like a river flowing of ecstasy

We're getting high just like you like
On this thing called life or something like
Oh did I say too much?
I'm sorry but I just can't get enough.

Laura Martin

HORSE IN THE RAIN

I saw her go out
That night around nine
The pretty girl in the bedsit
That's right above mine
And I spoke to her, asked her
If she was okay
But she just stared at me
In a very strange way
Until she replied
And she looked so forlorn,
'Bruised leaves and crushed petals
Hurt more than the thorn.'

Such a curious answer
Although, at the time
I was thinking, perhaps
It was part of a rhyme
As I watched her walk off
All alone in the rain
I wish I had known
She was circling the drain.
She was found the next morning
Devoid of all charm
Not a thorn, but a needle
Remained in her arm.

J. C. Fearnley

INDEPENDENCE

Have you ever had that sinking feeling
Which makes you all confused?
You realise you're on your own
Just waiting to be used
Life holds many untold secrets
When you find them it seems too late
You've just got up as it knocks you down
Never knowing why, you accept your fate
If life is there to be enjoyed
Why are there so many tests?
Who cares if we're strong or weak
Or better than the rest?
Why is it that when you think you're winning
You always end up last?
Has someone up there made a list
Of problems we all must task?
If this is how the world is run
The question has to be
Why do some people suffer
When others have it so easy?
Life is like a roulette wheel
You end up lucky or lose
Some people have gold and silver
Others are left with the blues
I often wonder while I'm alone
If we're really born for a reason,
You start as a baby then grow up
More independent with every season
Growing up is the easiest part
But as maturity sets in you get lost
Along the road you learn many things
Independence comes with a cost.

Michelle Holton

MANLY VALUES

Of course – it's all coming back now
The tottie with the heavenly jugs
At one of Jeff's get-togethers, right
Cock Fosters you say, yeah that rings a bell

Wasn't she with the weasel sporting the bow tie
No, you assume she came with Sam
By the way how is the bitch
Back in rehab, ah, bless her

Getting back to Ms Boobs Bountiful
If the old memory isn't playing tricks
I recall helping her with the sandwiches
Cut a bloody finger
What do you mean I should have been paying attention
That was the trouble
I was paying too much attention

Jesus, so near yet so far
The one that got away so to speak
Or should that be the two that got away
Story of my life, hombre

Anyhow, what about her
Dead, a car accident, you're kidding me
You're not kidding me
Shit, what a waste – did she have a name?

T Cobley

NO ONE WAS THERE

When I was born it was not fair, doctor
Midwife were not there.
I tell you mate it was a scare.
No one was there.
You may think this all strange and queer,
To have no one anywhere near,
Even my mother was having a beer.
No one was there.
As I stood at the altar's side, looking anxiously for my bride,
That was when I nearly cried
No one was there.
Walking down that country lane, suddenly I felt a pain,
I cried out loud all in vain.
No one was there.
Climbing up a very steep hill, I remembered not taking that pill,
As I lay so very still.
No one was there.
At my grave the vicar prayed, solitary figure that he made.
Friends, relation, flowers, delayed.
No one was there.
Surfing heaven on a cloud, wind a'whispering through my shroud.
Though I shouted very loud.
No one was there.
Hammering on St Peter's Gate, wondering what would be my fate.
All I did was wait, wait, wait and wait.
No one was there.
A little haunting I had to do, round old castles I once flew.
A hundred years without one 'Boo!'
No one was there.
This is my tale of a life and hereafter, a sorry tale that gets much dafter.
Because I can hear, the sound of laughter.
But no one is there.

Roy Hare

MY TWO LOVING ANGELS

My dear old mother and father
Are now both happily together
High up in Heaven above
But down here on Earth below
I can still feel all of their
Warm and tender love
And I know they will always
Be there for me
Should I ever need any advice
Or some warm and friendly company

So thank you dear Lord above
For those two loving parents
And all the joy and happiness
That they both gave to me
When we were all together
Down here on Earth below.

Donald Tye

A REFLECTION ON KITCHEN MAID AT EMMAUS BY VELASQUEZ

Have we not at times tried
To hide from our pain of him
In the backrooms of our lives?

Smelling the bread
Listening to the sight
And seeing the sound

Flooded with the way of new
From the dead
And the sombre evening candlelight.

James O'Grady

ODE TO ORANGE JUICE

I stand alone against a backdrop of broken rubble,
A ruby red liquid vanishing with every bubble,
I wonder to myself what I did to deserve such trouble,
Wishing my life had been that much more admirable.

I look across at my broken home,
And gaze in amazement as the pieces begin to roam,
Clasping together like a horse to a soam,
This beautiful combination of foam and chrome.

I feel my body pulling together and raising from the floor,
My aches and pains are vanishing and limbs are no longer sore.
I rise to the table with its legs now a set of four,
And watch as the empty frame recombines with the broken door.

I sense the touch of chrome and glass,
And smell the smell of freshly cut grass,
As I become a liquid mass,
And from the air to glass I pass.

The bright white light that once disturbed my dreams,
Begins to withdraw from the room in beams,
Taking with it the sound of shattered screams.
Allowing the world to be free of broken seams.

I sit upright feeling bold and proud,
And watch as the deadly mushroom cloud,
Retracts from the stare of the advancing crowd,
Returning the lives of those it ploughed.

I hear the sound of a retreating plane,
And the cheers of a city no longer in twain,
The heavy horn of a smoky train,
And the pitter-patter of summer rain.

I listen closely for a key in the door,
Waiting for footsteps to sweep the floor,
And I watch as they advance just like before,
Only this time a hand reaches forward ready to pour.

I await the gentle filling sound,
Of plastic and orange juice compound,
As it and I become rebound,
To once again feel profound.

I see a face with a gentle yawn,
Who wishes he hadn't got up this morn,
But little does he know of a brand new dawn,
Where mistakes and tears become withdrawn.

I settle myself as the lights go out,
Contented at surviving a terrible rout.

Shaun Anthony

THE CITY AT NIGHT

Now the nightclub's empty
Streets, littered with rubbish
Detritus, that escaped the bin
Neon's, stutter brokenly, flashing
Their unwanted, unwelcome message.

Silence now broken, by odd shouts
As late-goers, drift homeward
Lamps, move in wind, miscast shadows
Letters darkly gesture, in yellow paint
'No parking', either needed, or wanted.

Ozone, filters back exhaust gas
While, in subway (much beloved)
Of civic planners, lurid graffiti
Beckons in, innuendo and slander
Saving Facebook, harassment in court.

Silhouetted, denizens disrobe, as
One-by-one, window lights extinguish
Cats whine and patrol, restless
Walls, topped with broken glass
The city, hums into kilowatt slumber.

Adrian McRobb

LONDON

The sights, smells and sounds of London
Where our Queen's Coronation took place,
Which fills Londoners with pride.
With Royal palaces, pearly kings and queens.
Houses of Parliament, and impressive Big Ben.
Buildings steeped in History.
Some as though time had stood still.
The River Thames, with its bridges galore.
Added to the Docklands,
Just a few of the sights to see
With the Docklands light railway
With its efficiency.
London sets your heart pounding,
Wherever you may roam.
Buckingham Palace, is Her Majesty's home,
This year is special, it is the Queen's Jubilee.
So many will take part in the celebrations.
It will be part of history.
The Olympic Games are here,
People from all around the world,
Will want to see.
The Mayor of London,
The elected Government,
Have important decisions to make in everyday life.
Also there is the magnificent
Millennium Dome.
Its opening was the year two thousand
A remarkable achievement, adding to London pride.
Also fruit markets, fish markets, flower markets,
All adding interest, with bargains galore
London has so much to offer.
Covent Garden, the city,
Businessmen with their briefcases.
Also in a hurry.
Stock markets, with arms waving,
Stockbrokers on the floor
Watching the world markets
Sending shares, up and down, in a flurry.
Nelson's Column in Trafalgar Square, Leicester Square
Harrods, Selfridges, Liberty's,
High quality shops beyond compare.
All human life, walk on the streets of London.
All leading different lives, all nationalities are there.
The great London taxi and familiar

Double-decker red bus.
The Underground, all efficient, transporting,
All of us.
The Changing of the Guard,
With all of its pageantry,
With many people watching
It's a great sight to see.
Also beautiful parks, the Royal Albert Hall.
Individual's needs served,
With foods from all around the world.
They are beyond compare,
My opinion is,
That you have never lived until,
You have experienced London.
Visit it and you can guarantee,
Once you have been bitten by its bug;
The more you visit,
The more you will want to see.
It's not the place that you will easily forget.
Seeing is believing, experiencing London;
Filling your mind,
With an interest,
For all to share.
Museums, Art Galleries, Abbeys, Churches,
All are beyond compare.
Forgive me if I boast,
I am glad that I live there.
Here's hoping,
You will take the time to see,
London, because it is the place to be.
My heart beats in time
In this marvellous city.
With its interest, and beauty.
To see it,
Is every person's duty.

Sheila Booth

YOUR PET NAME WAS BUTTON, BUT ALL MY PETS ARE DEAD

My last girl
She was a cheater,
I haven't reacted to it
Like a *real* man
Perhaps keying obscene words;
Or a giant abstract cock
On her car door,
Or shitting a big brown stain
Into an innocent white envelope
Setting it alight – pressing it hard
Through the mail slot in her door
And watching her house self-destruct
Like she watched me
That night she uttered these words:
'I'm sorry. I've been with another man.'

I haven't reacted to it at all
Like a *real* man,
Instead
I imagine myself telling rooms of shared friends
That her vagina is the size
Of a condom
After an immature teenage boy
Has blown it up and put it over his head,
And that to initiate sex
I had to shout the secret word
Into her c**t, and listen out for permission
Echoed back by her cave monsters;
And sometimes, if I'm lucky, I'll get to dream
Of them both, their crooked liars' teeth trapped
Between two cars, a spark, and a petrol leak.

My last girl
She was a cheater
And I can't say that I've reacted to it
Like a *real* man
But a better man.

Craig Taylor-Broad

17TH FLOTILLA 25TH ANNIVERSARY

Dougie Penrith had an idea,
That brought old sailors together.
They came from far, they came from near,
No matter what the weather.

Without the trepidation,
They felt, when off to war.
But a feeling of elation,
As they met up again once more.

It is good to sit around,
Hear the tales they have to tell.
Although comradeship they found,
Some must have gone through hell.

So let us raise our glasses,
To the Navy and Jack Tar.
Pause a quiet moment,
For those who crossed the bar.

Enjoy the anniversary,
And although we have to part.
Memories and friendship,
Remain within the heart.

May God bless and keep you,
As you travel on your way
Friendships remain, strong and true,
'Til we meet again some day.

Peggy Howe

CRADLED AT HEART

She flies across the deserts of building sites
Over the stinking slums of the city dumps
And into the morgue of the knacker's yard

Beneath the mountains and valleys of dying cars
Squats an old bunker, once the play den of a child
Unseen posters line grey walls and hide the cracks
Blankets rot in the musty darkness of a frozen crypt

A lonely flash of colour as she alights upon a yellowed dome
And sees among those tiny arches, so delicately formed
So fit to line a cathedral or castle of kings, her nest of twigs
Her squalling brood of helpless infants keep a heart beating
Where a heart beat once before.

Katie Gisborne

GROWN-UPS CAN CRY

I said to my grandpa, when I was small
Who is that picture on the wall?
He ceased rocking, in his rocking chair
As with trembling hand, he stroked my hair.
I looked up and to my surprise
I saw tears, in my grandpa's eyes
That is your grandmother, my dear wife
The one, the only love of my life
She would have given you so much love
But the good Lord needed her above
Maybe his needed exceeded mine
To help him with his work divine
Grandpa resumed rocking in his chair
He had forgotten I was there
As I crept from the room, I lingered a while
I saw Grandpa give the sweetest smile
Before very long, I shall leave this strife
Keep a place beside you, love of my life
With an ache in my heart, I closed the door
I had never known grown-ups cry before
I discovered something new that day.
I will never forget it, come what may.

Iona Watt

ALL OUR YESTERDAYS

The clouds above go drifting by
There are no boundaries between Earth nor sky,
The age of light and dark is upon us,
We must fight this battle as one
But in the past we were someone,
Heroes of the hour
Yet now the long forgotten
Fallen heroes come together now.

All our yesterdays
All our hazy daze
To a past of a distant time,
Crossing futures with the chimes,
No matter what I try to do
Memories reflect you
To a time when I loved you
Walking beneath the brightest star
The past is fading from afar.

It seems that all our yesterdays
Have begun to dwindle and to fade,
You and I stood together,
But now we only have today.
What was once proud and gallant
Crumbles now to dust
Reflections of our past it appears,
Is now just nothingness.
I cry to God 'Oh why?'
Must all our yesterdays disappear
Seems to answer just in time
To wipe away a lonely tear.

Future doth reflect the past
In solemn unison we tried our path,
To a distant horizon that seems unattained.
The past is teacher to the present
To learn the lessons left behind,
Yet, why am I so empty now without your love
It doesn't seem to matter much
But destiny keeps on slowly revolving.
Into a future so uncertain
And all our yesterdays dissolving.

Richard Charles

THIS IS TRUTH

What is truth?
It is something you cannot touch,
You cannot hold it,
Yet truth was the same yesterday
The same today
And tomorrow it will not change.

What is truth?
Truth is a light in darkness
Truth is able to go
Into a grove of trees,
Kneel in faith,
And have faith rewarded with
Knowledge.

What is truth?
Truth is to be able to accept
That which touches your heart,
Stops you, and changed your thoughts,
Ways and actions.
Truth makes you a better man
Or woman
If you accept it.

What is truth?
Truth is the sunrise in the east,
Truth is the night following day.
Truth is a seed planted,
Watered, nurtured,
Reaching upward towards light
From Darkness.

What is truth?
Truth is trust between two or more persons,
Who knows no boundaries
When help is needed.
Truth has a price to be paid,
But not by money.

Truth is more precious that diamonds
Or gold,
For truth can purchase for you
Those things that are not available
To those who are financially wealthy.

What is truth?
I am that I am this is truth,
The Saviour's eyes are truth,
His footsteps lead the way to truth,
His actions are truth.

Oh, where is truth?
Truth is all around us
As we observe all nature,
Placed on Earth for us all.
Truth is available to all.
None are exempt,
Black, white or brown.

Truth is to speak without a forked tongue.
There are no shades of truth,
Truth is truth at all times,
Truth replaces fear and doubt.

What is truth?
Truth is all these things and many more.
Truth is a gift given to us
To explore ourselves,
Our universe, our world.
Truth is eternal,
And when you find it,
Treasure it.

George Aspinall

THE NEW ADDITION

Many speculations of who
Will be Wills' bride
Were wild and furious
But Wills is now happy with Kate at his side

We feel Wills has chosen wisely
Wild guesses proved quite an adventure
His contentment obvious
With his Kate completing the picture.

Two peas in a pod
Kate accompanying Wills' every exhibition
The royal family look even more royal
And sedate, with Kate as the new addition.

With Kate and Wills to take over
It's a welcome from in-law, our Queen
It is calming as our royalty
Has never actually been.

Barbara Sherlow

MODERATION

When you have been in the house for a while, isn't it nice to go out?
When you have been out a while, it's good to get home.
After you have been sitting a while, it's nice to stand.
When you have stood for too long, to rest your legs is the general plan.
When you feel so hot, it is nice to cool your toes.
When you are so cold, it is nice to warm, this is how the scheme of things goes.
The best idea, is everything in moderation,
To keep things just about right, is the best solution.
Eat when you are hungry, drink to quench your thirst.
But do not eat until you could burst.
Drink just enough for your personal needs.
Then you will find you can carry out your deeds.
Enjoy life, but don't go mad.
Think about others, try to be good, not bad.
You will find, as years go by,
You can face most things life hands out to you,
With a twinkle in your eye.

Yvonne Chapman

SPOILED MORNING

Dust motes dancing in shafts of light
Piercing the blinds, heralds the end of night
Minutes tick by on bedside alarm
Rise from your slumber from bed still warm

Greet the world and start your day
Would you have it any other way?
Washed and dressed, down for toast
Coffee too, it smells like fresh roast

Day is starting up all around
Radio gives that background sound
Then off to work it's not too far
Shall I walk? No take the car.

Driving off and all feels great
Best get moving, can't be late
Speeding truck skids round the bend
Didn't expect that . . . *bang!* That's the end.

Ken Capps

MINIMUM WAGE

I sweep with a brush
And grab awkward weeds
To put in a black plastic bag.
Why do I do the same hours?
Bloody wrong!
Gaffer gone good.
Why someone work next to me
Paid more money?
Bloody wrong!
I throw down brush,
Dump out black plastic bag,
Sit down.

Martin Holmes

ALONE

Standing alone, a soul in the dark
Just an empty space, for a friend
Spinning thoughts around in your head
Making no sense, beginning to end.

Just wanting company, a voice to reply
To the questions, you're wanting to ask
A friendly ear, a listening device
Somebody, to see beyond the mask.

Your mind plays tricks, when you are alone
Imagination, can run wild and free
Seeing pictures, images, real and false
Such distortion, is all that you see.

Watching the time, the sound of the clock
Ticking, so deafening to your ears
Concentration, so hard, mind tends to roam
Many days and nights, filled with tears.

Hopefully your soul, will find a friend
And a shoulder, to carry the pain
A person to love and take care of
And to make life worth living again.

Richard Morris

GYMFIX

If life's worry wear you down; one's lined
Face, complexions frown.
If limb twinge of aching pain, leaves you
Pondering why the strain?
Can't seem to rise above slight colds, or
Weary thoughts you're growing old.
Find gym funds! Pump heart and lungs; exercise,
Take prudent plunge.

No medic's note would certify, or give alarm
False reason why?
When after check and all reads clear, he sees
No risk to interfere.
Aerobics fine! Why waste vain time on medication's
Costly dime?
Put sound mind to moving parts, and soonest sign a start.

Some will say no need for that; argue, theroy's words fall flat.
Others try, but won't succeed, while wise ones
Know beneficial need.
Nothing daunts keyed one who's keen, results of
Which will soon be seen.
Fitter body! Fitness find, drives delusion from
Vague mind.

Accept down days you'd never train!
Flu needs rest; viral strains do drain!
Reluctant feet from chair or bed, decline to go
Where they would tread.
Motivation you'll soon need, regive muscle fibres feed.
Exercise is what most need! Regardless of cliqued creed.

David Pooley

LOW-BUDGET SCI-FI PUBERTY

Is that the sound a laser makes?
Or do balls make that sound while sinking?

And it's not me squeaking
And it's not me growling
It's some kind of mechanical fault
With the gun
Or the dry ice machine

Zap!
And now you've come too close
In search of a laddish insult
And gone and made
Yourself an easy target

Your all-JJB plus Dalek outfit
Vibrating like an effusive
Ann Summer's event
If we knew what one of them
Was then

My enemies' perverse curiosity
May just be my
First glory in this game
Of the future as visualised by the 1990s . . .

This ain't the kind of battlefield
Where the warriors of yore
Came of age
But it'll have to do

Yeah we are easily entertained
In this era;
We still feel fear in shitty
Labyrinths in provincial retail parks

But this conspiracy of scrotum
And larynx
Is far more terrifying
Than anything Centre 4 can muster

Shouldn't have come here
When the first throaty twinges came
Should've waited out the afternoon
In with my mum watching 'Goldfinger'

Because if Connery-era Bond
Taught us anything it's that
Lasers and testicles are not compatible.

Gary From Leeds

THE GARDEN

A garden is a pleasure
Especially when open to the public;
All may enter, enjoy is blessings
Municipal or private, ownership irrelevant;
Adequate maintenance essential.
The public and/or private purse
Is not misspent on grass, flowers, plots, shrubs, trees.

Public parks and gardens, open spaces,
With joys of colour, form and texture,
Changing with the seasons,
Residence and sanctuary for wildlife,
Renew the spirit, uplift the heart,
Give peace, freedom and contentment –
Saving graces for troubled lives and living;

An open door, an open gate,
To the wonders of the world, creation –
Evidence of a new dimension,
A break in space and time,
Where balance and perspective is regained
On the affairs and politics of life and living!

Ian Forrester

SUMMER HOLIDAY

My landlady's Martha
Her husband is Arthur
I spend each day by the sea
The ice cream's inviting
The pier is enticing
With buttered scones served up for tea

I went to see Sadie
Billed as the fat lady
Who clearly lived life to the full
I sent Mum a postcard
The verse by a coarse bard
About a saucy young lass by a pool

The sun shines brightly
I dance almost nightly
The lager glides down like a treat
And daily I play
The amusement arcade
Or gaze at the sea from a seat

When I freeze in December
I'll still remember
This fortnight of ease by the sea
As I trudge down the street
Bombarded by sleet
I'll still feel the sun shines on me.

Stuart Delvin

BRITAIN GREAT

People think we're not so great
Not to laugh or take the bait
The Jubilee and our Queen
Then the Olympics yet to be seen
England is a country that's proud
Negativity is not allowed
Think about good, dismiss the bad
We won the war, just ask your dad
We'll, be great again if we take a stand
God save the Queen, and our land!

Elizabeth Corr

RIVALS - POETRY AND POVERTY

Poetry and poverty
Two words which seem the same
With that V the only difference
A valley in-between
Poor people on either side
Claiming to be both
With pubs and hard luck stories
We go through all the crowds
Poverty and poetry
Seeking something that isn't real

How I love her
Let me count the way
My heart beats like the night
Empty until appearing like the moon
Her pale face fills me with light
Stars dance upon us both
Swaying like strands of corn
Beside a silent river
There I compare her

Running down to the sea
Pulling me helpless
Go now with the tide
I drown in an ocean of passion
Soul forever in chains
Slave to her adoration
Could never love anyone more
She leaves me breathless with emotion
Washed up on devotions shore

Yes there is poetry in poverty
But seems to be much
More poverty in poetry
Can I sell you this for the
Price of a bottle of Remy Martin?

Rodger Moir

MY LIFE, MY TIME, MY SPACE

Don't shuggle the accumulator, said with elation
Or you'll shake up every station.

Wireless, television, Internet
Man's thirst for knowledge, barely met.

Early days the Goons, the glums
Earlier still the wartime drums.

Dum, dum, dum, dum
Music adapted to thwart the Hun
Coded music not for fun.

BBC with worldwide coverage
English spoken, Malcolm Muggeridge.

Ying Tin Yakara poo spurtin'
Drama. Under Milk Wood, Burton.

Financial disaster, the Wall Street Crash
Wiped us out, depression on the backlash.

The Empire Exhibition, king and queen, very grand
Me on Dad's shoulder, flag in hand.

King George's death, Edward to reign?
Fate stepped in to rule again.

Abdication, solemn and bland
Edward and Simpson, hand in hand.

Thirties teetering on the brink
Chamberlain-Hitler, salute don't think.

Clydebank Blitz, bombs raining down
Slaughtering innocents, bloodied ground.

Evacuation, shunted out of town
Frantic scramble, gone to ground.

Holocaust, Atom bomb, rations
Nylon stockings, New Look fashions.

Greenham Common, the pill, the coronation
Women's voices rebuilding the nation.

Sixites people flower power
Vietnam War, Napalm shower.

Musical London in all its glory
Kismet, Hair, West Side Story.

Festival of Britain, showtime at last
Wartime behind us an icy blast.

Catherine Hislop

THE WOODS

There is magic in the woods
Of secret mists and shadows deep
That lurk and dart among the trees
To bless our thoughts and fill our hearts.

There is a silence in the woods
Of lonely phantoms – muted dreams,
Aromas of dank pungent smells
That fill our nostrils and our mind.

There is a whispering in the woods
Of murmuring streams and muffled moans,
Lamenting longings – ancient rhymes
That stir the leaves and shrubs therein.

There is a singing in the woods
Of sighs and groans that breezes bring
Where bough and branch do hang their heads
Inhaling sorrows of our souls.

There is a magic in the woods
Of healing balms that do abound
To take confessions of our sins
To cleanse our spirits, to set us free.

Lesley Francis

MY MAGIC ROOM

In my magic bright red room
Are loads and loads of toys
Waiting there to have some fun
With all you girls and boys.

Jumping frogs who hop all night
And many coloured balls
And china men with slanting eyes
And lots and lots of toys
A lovely ballerina
Who dances round the floor
There's tigers, lion and monkeys too
And many, many more.

A circus clown with large pink shoes
Jumps all about the place
And all the toys just have to laugh
When looking at his face
There's acrobats and elephants
And bears and giraffes too
And teeny weeny spiders
Crawling in and out of shoes.

There's soldiers in green uniforms
With buttons shining bright
Marching up and down the room
They really are a sight
I'm sure you'd all enjoy yourselves
Amongst those lovely toys
And they would be so happy
To meet you girls and boys.

John Wilson Dennison

THE CRYSTAL MAZE

When we start out on our long, last journey
The road will be rough and so black,
But after the body has thrown off its shackles
Then a change will take place to this heavenly track.

Slowly the dark disappears altogether
And the sun will start to break through,
And far in the distance we see a bright light
As a crystal maze comes into view.

When caught in the maze we reflect on our life,
Each wrong turn we make is because of a sin,
And as we pass through, we can look on ourselves
As we twist and we turn for the exit to win.

And when we emerge from this glittering maze
And go through the labyrinth gate,
We can see before us the entry to Heaven
For in there we will find out our fate.

And now there is only one hurdle to climb,
The one that appears on the Judgement Day,
When the Lord of all Lords and the King of all Kings
Shall tell us whether we're doomed or can stay.

Elizabeth Zettl

AN EXPENSIVE HOBBY

I have always enjoyed sending letters,
To all my relations, and friends,
But the latest rise, in postage stamps,
Means my hobby, now ends.
I'll have to stop, sending Christmas cards,
And maybe, birthday cards too,
Also stop sending a holiday postcard,
With a wonderful view,
No more sending, thank you cards,
So I hope, my friends, will understand,
That I did appreciate their gifts,
And thought, they were really grand.
Now posties will be quite worried,
About how long, their jobs will last,
And lots of letters, will end up in museums,
As 'Antiques of the past'.

Jean Hendrie

BEING THERE . . .

Hold this moment
Freely given –
Life's enchantment
Onward driven.
Bless the way
That all unfolds . . .
The orchestration
We can behold.
If life is spent
In doing, not being
His majesty
We are not seeing.
To touch, to feel
A love, so pure
Is his design . . .
Of that – I'm sure.

Edith Wise

ME MA

She was born to John and Annie
They christened her Elizabeth Josephine
She was so beautiful
She was named again Lilly
You would love to see her
Mother Teresa did
She was one out of the 22 her mother had who survived
Lilly was on her way to follow suit
Instead she got a coloured, TV, stronger windows and a new lock on herr door
And through me da out for good
She notched up 16 pregnancy
And had a 11 births, one didn't stay long
Marion moved above to channel down grace
Thought if you heard, seen or felt half the things us 12 experience together
You probably say what grace
A, but only we know their was grace in-between the events
We're all still letting in air accept me poor Olefella
My ma gave me a gift for life
She had me at home
Up on the top balcony in our flat, 308
No Norse or Doctor to label me
Just her and her neighbour Maggie Burn
The first human I open my eyes to was my beautiful mother Lilly
And since that beautiful image
Me have never seen an ugly woman and never will
There isn't one in the universe
From the first to arrive to the last who leaves
And that was my mother's gift to me
Thanks Ma Lilly.

John Walsh

A DAY OF THE LIFE IN MY 80S

Monday's quite a busy day –
Fun and frolics all the way.
'Dial-a-ride' is at my door,
Smiles from the driver,
'Blip! Blip!' the seat belt.
Out with my money,
She asks how I've felt.
My 'walker' is stowed away
Off to keep fit!

Now for a jolly hour
Moving all parts –
Feet, legs and bodies,
Arms, back and strong hearts,
Each doing her best with a
Smile of good cheer.

What a relief – here comes a drink,
Oh! It's only water – well, what did you think?
No time to ponder, so much to do.
If you can't do it all,
Just do your best
Still more to activate,
No time to rest.
Whew! That was hard
Why did I join?

At last it's all over,
Now out to the bus,
The driver's returned and she's
Waiting for us.

In next to no time
She's dropped me at home.
That beaker of coffee
Goes down a treat,
Then my 'walker and I'
Are back up the street.

A brief ride in the bus
And a welcome meal,
A short haircut and wave
And it's home once again.

The busy day has more to come –
It's 'Open sight' at 7:30
Off we go to the club.

There's entertainment, snacks and chats.
Golly! I've won the raffle again
Home we go!
What a full day!

Stephanie Stone

ALWAYS

'Will you still love me when I'm old and grey?
When my teeth are no longer my own?
When I'm all weather-worn, having lived better days
When the years like the birds have flown?

Will you still love me when my twilight has come?
When my youth has gone down the pan?
When my beauty, for surely I must have some
Is replaced by a wrinkly woman?

Will you still love me when my sight fades dim?
When my hearing is greatly impaired?
When it's difficult to manoeuvre without my zim
And I struggle to get up the stairs?

Will you still love me when my legs fall weak?
When they spring forth varicose veins?
When it's all I can muster to even speak
Without any aches and pains?

Will you still love me when I need you the most?
When I've bade goodbye to my health?
When I'm one shuffle away from the Paradise Coast.
And unable to care for myself?

Will you still love me my dearest Ted
When my memory becomes just a haze?'
And he placed a finger to her lips and said,
'My dearest Dotty . . . Always.

Peter Terence Ridgway

WE'RE ALL LIKE SNOWFLAKES

Just before you plummet
Recall the season in the sun
Where getting to the summit
Wasn't as hard as it was fun
Just passing time
As it's passed me
The aging crime
Don't come free
The skeleton aches
Flesh loses the tone
Standard time takes
All your youth has known
Shattered time in scattered rhymes
Is as bleak as the hardest frost
An shattered rhyme in scattered times
Comes at one helluva cost
Still hanging on in there
Got the tiger by the tail
Holding the leg of a bear
In the mouth of a killer whale
The fiddle you play is second
Causing your soul to sigh
It's a reckoning we don't reckon
Living in the storms eye
Right now it's in torment
Titanic in it's allure
Ain't nothing you can do to prevent
The ice clear clarity of failure
Seen things come to be
The succeeding an losing
Life's joy an' misery
Fates twisted collusion
So your stuck in the middle
From the day you are born
Life will always be a riddle
As farmer time harvests it's corn
Your so fed up
Feel like you could bust
Your dreamers cup
Is full of broken dream dust
Everyone tires getting put down
You got to keep getting up
Continue swimming not to drown
Thristy for adventure then sup

It's a long tiring flight
When the bird loses its song
To stay it's a fight
Feeling you don't belong
So heavy in blame
Always seem to be wrong
Saturated in shame
We know how the bird lost its song
Take you into insanity
Borderline you've free-wheeled
Selfish pride an vanity
Is a destructive minefield
So mind where you walk
Life's steps ain't always free
An' remember cheap talk
Sometimes it comes with a fee
Born to lose
Though you're dying to win
Hang dog hound blues
Howl under the skin
Won't leave you alone
Like a ravenous thirst
Turn you to stone
Like your Medusa cursed
You bend an' break
It's always been the way
I hope when you ache
Your pain quickly goes away
We all make mistakes
Not one person could deny
We're all like snowflakes
We flurry, drift, settle, melt an die
Sometimes you hurt when you care
There's pain within compassion
When burdens with others we share
Remember everyone needs a bastion
All of us have to suffer
Some a lot more than others
It's not a case of just get tougher
When you're broken already sisters an' brothers
Just keeps on going
An' can't recall why
Just keeps on showing
Where the truth does lie
Ain't wanting to look for a spade
To dig deeper into sorrow

Even though through negatives we wade
Today is only a yesterday of tomorrow.

Mark Tough

THE GARDEN IN MID-WINTER

The Winter sky in the morning
Is orange, gold and red
After a night of piercing, hoary frost
On the grass and each flower bed.

The roses, that before were so fine and bright,
Hang their heads but are still alive
While the azaleas, marigolds and such
Are all fighting to survive.

The bitter cold winds of previous days
Have denuded the trees of their leaves
So now, in the roofs of warm houses,
The birds come to roost in the eaves.

The pond looks so drab now the lilies,
That gave such a show summer-long,
Have melted away 'neath the water
And ice seals them in where they've gone.

However, there's hope in the garden,
The bulbs are poking their tips through the earth
And the primulas, pansies and aconites
Are blooming to prove their worth.

The snowdrops, crocus and jonquils
Will put on their marvellous show
And it won't be long before daffodils
Brighten the place with their glow.

Tulips and iris and cowslips
Will be waiting there, in the wings,
To take their place till the bedding plants
Will fill the garden in Spring.

Fredrick West

LAMENT FOR A LOST BILLIARD HALL

There was a place quiet and green
And happy hours we spent.
Old friends to keep us on our feet,
We borrowed and we lent.
When we were young and lean.

And older generations and sibling relations
Passed on their skill and with a will
Displayed their expertise or cloaked it with great ease.
And egotists were taken down
And humble men could wear the crown.

For those, who went before us
Would tell us all in chorus
That hustling was necessitous
For them; it not for us.

And in the clicking quiet hush;
Beneath the shaded lights,
Many was the formal brush,
And sometimes there were fights.

A lifetime later that quiet green
Is still around and can be seen.
No more the take down of the mugs;
Now it houses carpets and rugs.

The Luciana Billiard Hall
As such went to the wall.
The young lions of its salad days
Are scattered on their many ways.

The old guys had a misspent youth,
But were not mugging yobs,
When war restored prosperity,
(Save for a small minority)
They held down jobs and that's the truth.

Bill Looker

JESS

Our life was changed forever the day that Jess was born
The children came home so happy, yet a little bit forlorn
They told me Judy had puppies all wet and very thin
But Judy licked and cleaned them and made them all look trim
They asked me oh so sweetly, full of innocence and charm
Could they please have a puppy so tiny and so warm
At first I said a firm *no.* Well that was a waste of breath
You've guessed, they got their puppy, to save her from certain death
When they brought the tiny bundle she was golden brown like corn
They popped her in the basket, somehow she knew this was home
She cried for a while for her mother, but they gave her so much love
She soon forgot and started to settle down by the stove
The mess and all the puddles only lasted a little while
Even while she was still learning we couldn't help but smile
At the funny little antics and expressions on her face
As she trotted out to the garden with a certain charm and grace
Time passed as time is bound to and Jess is now full grown
Her place within this family is simply number one
She has us all well measured and knows just what to do
To keep us all attentive and make us happy too
She lies curled up in her basket and yet keeps a careful watch
And woe betide the stranger who dares our door to touch
There never was a greeting more noisy than one from Jess
She barks and growls at strangers, as a guard dog she's the best
When you reach up for her leader hung on the special hook
She rushes round excited then stops to wait and look
One of her greatest pleasure is going for a walk
Trotting along beside you and sniffing at every stalk
Her eyes speak as no voice can and when she tilts her head
You know just what she's asking thought not a word is said
Just reach out for a chocolate and you have got a friend
Sharing every mouthful right to the very end
She loves her tummy tickled and playing with her toys
Her games go on forever and tires out the boys
Her idea of heaven is to curl up on your knee
I'm sure she thinks it's her chair and she's lending it to me
She's devoted to this family and will wait for ever more
When left out in the garden she just sits outside the door
Our Jessy is a baby when it comes to bathing too
She hates the soapy water and sadly looks at you
Sweet-smelling and all dripping she runs out to the grass
She shakes herself all over and leaves an awful mess
If anyone had told me a few short years ago
A dog could change our household in a way we'd never known

I wouldn't have believed you, in fact I would think you spoke in jest
But that was before we'd lived with this little dog called Jess.

We lost Jess when she was seventeen years old and we miss her very much.

Jean Rawson

FEAR

It's absolutely paralysing
It drives you to do things out of mind
It drives you to run
It drives you to fight
It drives you to freeze
It drives you into utter pain, confusion, despair
It also makes you become secretive
It wants you to hide
It's like the Devil crouching behind every corner
It destroys trust
It builds heaps of mistrust
It disappoints
It hates
It makes cowards
But, if only once you display love, trust and calm,
Then all of the above crumbles into nothing, as fear can't live on a courageous heart.

Isla Demuth

PLEA FROM THE DEER

Across my vision
Barely camouflaged, they glide
Tan-white, black-red
Graded are their dapple hides
Their supple flanks a-ripple
With muscle half-hidden
Their hindquarters subtly shaded
Like fragments from a waking dream they slide
Branched antlers dark against the gilding sun
Heads bowed, like ancient supplicants
They drink from sun-annointed streams
I dare not, I cannot, approach
Instead I stand, feeling within a heart
Suddenly full-wise beyond my years
Their gaze of sad reproach
Tread carefully, do not disturb
This place was ours before men came
They seem to say
You cannot know, you cannot understand
Our need for sanctuary
Within these timeless lands
Of gorse, of bluebell, of the purple ling
You do not wake as we, with
The sun's red rising in the sky
You do not feed at leisure beneath
The shadow of the curlew's wing
Centuries pass, marking for our kind
Each generation of fawn, of stag, of gentle hind
Do not disturb, tread softly, leave us now to solitude
You may return to visit, but go
And look with wiser eyes upon the realms of humankind.

Sheila Sharpe

HOPE

I was only half alive before I met you,
I had give up all hope of ever meeting you that I could barely cope,
But then beyond that hope,
You came into my dreams your haunting melody,
Your gentle voice the soul of a poet it gave me feeling
And when we met you made me complete,
Bringing life back into me again,
My dream lover and true life-mate you know every part of me
Let my strong arms protect you,
Let me sing you to sleep,
Let me stand by your side and let me set your heart free,
I would never betray you for this love is forever,
In this life and the next,
You are the very heart of me look at me now,
See yourself through my eyes,
The most beautiful woman on this Earth
The perfect woman of my dreams,
My very own amazing gift beyond words

Guthrie Morrison

GOLDEN RULES

Departing with a wistful smile
Knowing there were many miles
Distance now was to separate
Just like a locked garden gate
Months and hours wrapped in dreams
Captured in invisible seams
Devoted were we in that enchanting chalet
A mystical attitude takes on a new bond
As we renounced to travel on
Leaving a flower-bedecked garden
With favourite walks and familiar vistas
Growing mature in a once family enclosure
Now in life's exposure
Cascades of fragrant plants over walls and pools
Leaning over with untidy tools
Gone are the golden rules.

Valerie Frances Mathew

BLUEPRINT - SHIP - ICE

(2012 - In memory of the Titanic, and passengers that sank 100 years ago.)

IT IS a modern mariner,
And he stoppeth only me.
'By thy short grey beard and penetrating eye
Now wherefore stopp'st thou me?'

The office doors are opened wide,
And I am next to be called in
The boss is there, the board is there:
May'st hear my heart beating.

He holds me with his damp hand,
'There was a ship,' quoth he.
'Hold off! Unhand me, grey-beard loon!'
Surprised, his hand dropt he.

He holds me with his penetrating eye
The ship designer stood still,
And listens like a three years' lamb;
The boss mariner hath his will.

The ship designer sat upon a chair;
He cannot choose but hear.
And thus spoke on that modern man,
The gloomy-eyed modern mariner.

The ship has been jeered, the harbour cleared.
Our shares they did drop
Below the FTSE, below the DOW,
Below the world's top.

The gloom came up upon the left,
Out of the tea came pain!
And out has gone our light
Down; down it has gone, out of sight!

'You designed the ship,' said he
'From mast to broom, eight till noon.'
The ship designer stood with beating heart,
For he felt like a loud buffoon.

The ice hath taken our ship to the wall,
Red as a rose felt he.
Nodding their heads were the board
With no sign of merry minstrelsy.

The ship designer had lost all sense of jest,
Yet he cannot choose but hear;

And thus spoke on that modern man,
The gloomy-eyed modern mariner.

And now the storm-blast came,
And he was tyrannous and long.
He struck with his o'ertaking swings,
And chastised the designer long.

With swinging arms and dripping nose,
He pursued with yell and blow.
And forward bends his head,
The modern mariner roared fast and loud,
The designer wishing he were dead.

And now there came a peaceful low
And he grew wondrous cold;
And ice, mast-high came floating by,
As green as emerald bold.

And through the drifts he saw snowy shifts
That did send a dismal sheen;
Nor shapes of men but beasts he ken
The ice was all between.

The ice was here, and bears were there;
The ice was all around.
He growled and roared in despair,
Like noises in a mound!

At length did cross his despairing mind,
Through the fog it came;
That his Christian soul was dead
So he hailed in God's name to be kind.

That this modern mariner recompense,
To a psychiastrist he must go;
His life from now submerged and dense,
The company and board on full slow.

PART 2

I wandered lonely in my grey shroud
As I floated on high o'er vales and hills,
When all at once I saw a crowd,
A host, of golden spirituals;
Beside the lake, all on their knees,
Singing and chanting beneath the trees.

I was lost among these stars that shine
As if part of the Milky Way.
This crowd stretched in never-ending line

Along the margin of a field of hay:
Thousands saw me in one glance,
Joy and love flowed from our new soul romance.

My shroud was grey, golden were they
They out-did me with waves of glee;
A dead designer could not but be gay,
In such a golden joyous company
I gazed – and – gazed and knew their thought
What wealth this crowd to me had brought.

For oft, when in my new sphere I may cry
They wash away my pensive mood,
Which is created by my one time solitude,
And then my heart with pleasure fills,
And dances with the spirituals.

Ron Atkin

REVOLVING DOORS

She left my heart behind closed doors
Then she moved on to other doors
She liked the thought of closing doors
Especially when I was behind those doors
I always hear the sound of closing doors
Especially when she slams the doors
My smile was left behind closed doors
Then she moved on to other doors
She had something about left-handed doors
Then she had something about right-handed doors
She had something about revolving doors
And then one day she couldn't find my door
She got lost in a revolving door

My sunshine smile is behind closed doors
I left my smile behind closed doors
One day she walked passed my door
She got lost in a revolving door.

David Rosser

THE COMPETITION

'I'll show you mine if you show me yours'
Said Fred to Tom as they sat in the back row
The judge down the front said, 'Shut up you two
Or out of the front door you will go'
Fred and Tom hung their heads in shame
Getting told off in front of your friends
'Maybe ours might not be big enough
surely that would make some amends.'

The judge called the first man up, 'Now lad
Slap it right down on the table'
Turned to the secretary, 'Please write it down
That's if you think you are able'
Out came the tape measure and rulers
The calipers, protractors and such
He then declared, 'It's twelve inches long
Five inches around and very smooth to touch.'

Murmurs went round, 'Twelve inches long'
That would take some beating
Bottoms shifted around uneasily
On the old-fashioned wooden bench seating
The next man strutted to the front
Placed his down very proudly
When the judge said, 'Eighteen inches'
The audience cheered very loudly.

Six men went before Fred and Tom
Pretty soon it would be their turn
Twenty-five pounds the prize was
They would have money to burn
Fred was called up in front of his wares
The judge shouted, 'Twenty-one inches'
And the audience stood on their chairs.

Tom was next, he drew himself up tall
And showed the judge what he'd got
The judge shouted, 'Twenty-two inches'
Our Tom had beaten the lot
The judge held up the silver goblet
For the biggest cucumber he'd seen
Tom just stood their proud as punch
Holding his cucumber so green.

Dorothy Fuller

2012

These days that we reside in
Are troubled much indeed
We see so much corruption – money – power – greed
The system is now failing
The Earth now falls apart
But still the masses sleep on
Unaware about the dark.

How sorrowful and weeping to see the life force die
Mankind became a parasite and sucked the planet dry
Through apathy it happened while the masters pulled the strings
Like puppets all the people danced to the tunes they singed.

But soon this time and space will pass
As a cleansing will begin to wipe the being of evil deed
Remorsed and full of sin.
We had a chance to make it a most beautiful a realm – a paradise –
A heaven – not this wicked hell.

All animals and creation that share this world with man
Have suffered with injustice as we destroyed the land
The seas now full of poison and toxic air we breathe
People need to realise how deep we've been deceived.

Many now awaken to the truths as we perceive
That we have been imprisoned here for elitist selfish deeds.
We all must join together now and bring back love and light
Exposing all the beasts that roam in the shadows of the night
Return Mother Earth to beauty and balance for us all
For the creator will soon call us as we hear the trumpet of call
So as we bow our heads in sorrow at the folly of our ways
Repenting for forgiveness or it will soon be end of days.

Chris Bampton

MARKET

Every Sunday morning, in sunshine or in rain
I'd rush off to a market, known as Petticoat Lane;
There join the crowds jostling through row upon row of stalls,
Watched the antics of stallholders, amused by their calls.

One chap sold dud watches for as much as they would pay,
'There's a mug born every minute,' he'd been heard to say,
Or 'They're not likely to come back, they come from far and wide,'
Though it is true there were a few who had the nerve and tried.

The 'China King' put on a show, juggled plates all morning long,
Never chipped or broke one, as proof that they were strong.
Is he still there, China in air? I really do not know,
For I last saw him more than seventy years ago.

Three 'Find the Lady' chancers were usually about,
One well behind the crowd, acting as their lookout;
One posing as a punter who naturally won the game,
Followed by fools who thoughts they could do the same.

Medicine Man could always draw the gullible and naïve,
His Elixir a perfect cure for any ill you can conceive;
It may indeed have helped a few, with the power of the mind.
There really is no end to the folly of mankind.

There were flypitchers lurking all along the street;
One was selling stockings, which seldom had two feet!
Sometimes I bought pretty beads from a fellow with a tray,
But only if they were at a price I could afford to pay.

Pricne Monolulu strode about, what an amazing sight
His flowing robes, feathers on head, made a dull day bright.
'I've got a horse, I've got a horse' he'd call out very loud
As he sold hot tips to gullible gamblers strolling in the crowd.

Sometimes as I sit dreaming, alone in my armchair,
I find myself imagining I am once again back there,
Pushing my way through those crowds without end,
With a pocketful of pennies I can't wait to spend.

Sarah Lindsay

THE TRAIN RIDE TO HELL

Doors bang, boots sound on the stairs,
Shouts of 'Out, out' and again 'Out, out,'
'Get your coats on, and get your bags,
Today all of you are moving house.'

Out in the street lined against a wall,
Then marched in ranks and lines of four
To the Ghetto, and then to the station
To catch a train, to you know not where.

The guards shout, 'Get on board, get on board,
The train is about to depart,
You are going on a long, long holiday
That will surely bless your heart.'

They travelled in trucks as carriages,
Three days, four days or maybe five.
When reaching their destination
Some were dead, and others were alive.

The sky was crying with great drops of rain
As the train finally came to stop.
The passengers alighted and walked towards a gate.
Unaware that death was their fate.

There was no joy of heart or singing,
Just the children crying and clinging
To their fathers and mothers as they wait,
For death while standing there at the gate.

Old people walked off to the right,
Young ladies were led straight ahead
While the young men went to the back
Of the station to their home, a shed.

Young children went to see the doctor,
Never to see or meet their folks again.
This was the main place of selection,
A point of great fear and awful dread.

Suitcases and luggage on the platform
Waiting to be reclaimed at a later date
Was another lied to add to all of the others.
Nothing was reclaimed by the people from that train.
They went to the ovens to become human remains.

John Harrold

GLADDIES

I thought I'd put some lilies
On this little card for you,
Paper white, and stately,
Not many, just a few,
Then I thought, I don't think so,
For, no matter what folk say,
Lilies may be elegant – but,
They don't chase your 'Blues' away!

But 'Gladdies,' they are different,
And point up to the sky,
As 'tho' they know our Lord's up there,
In His Heaven, up there on high,
And 'Gladdies' smile at everyone,
They take away the gloom,
Fresh bright colours, dazzling,
They brighten any room!

And so I pray these lovely flowers
Will help to lift your sorrow,
And bring some peace into your heart,
So that you can smile tomorrow.

Lucy D Williams

THE HONEY WAGON

Quick, close all the windows
Don't let that *smell* in here
For over the back field,
The honey wagons appeared
That thick dank known liquid
The farmer thinks it's great
But us poor city dwellers,
It's something that we hate
The smell is something awful
It creeps in everywhere
Get out the scented candles
That perfume we'll all share.

Liz O'Brien

AM I EVER?

Am I ever going to find
Someone who likes
Walking in the rain,
Somebody who feels
A sense of gratitude
For being alive
Just by watching
The clouds in the sky,
A being who satisfies his hunger
By breathing in the scent of flowers,
Someone who enjoys
The gentle breeze
Which seems to caress our faces,
Somebody who enjoys
Sitting on a bench by the river
And watch it flowing past,
No words spoken,
Only the murmur of our souls?

Noris D'Achille

IVY - WHO SERVED HER COUNTRY

What have you come through?
What have you seen?
Life in its raw state,
In places you've been.
Wartime, you lived through,
With comrades so brave,
Sitting at breakfast,
With some who were saved.
Bombs, air raids and Spitfires,
Lancasters and crew,
Whose engines and spark plugs
Depended on you.
Planes which you worked on
So Luftwaffe could fall,
We now have our freedom
It's thanks from us all.

Dorothy Baylis

BEREAVED

You cannot hold a mirror to my father's grief
You cannot see how the pain is fathoms deep
On your scale you cannot weigh the loss
While the world goes on he stands still always looking back at the life he left behind
Cruelly time has altered his beloved inalterably
He cannot pretend that what is bears any relation to what was
The cherished dream of her beauty and their shared love
Has become as much life's torment as life's consolation
For he must watch as she fades into total forgetfulness and indifference
Enveloped in the fog of senility
Yet my father stands proud, defiant
Anchored to a belief that to others seems a mirage
He refuses to cower in the face of time's destructive power
You watch him scream inwardly and hold his hand to lead him to tomorrow
To a land of no sorrow where his faith in the past will be redeemed.

Mónica Gurney

I DOUBT IT

If there's a god then let it be that he reveals himself to me,
My doubt has troubled me but yet it's not just something to forget
The image that I had, imprinted, etched upon my heart
Was placed there by my family and not decision on my part.

Eventually it came about, I knew I had to think it out,
Well what a task I set myself to place God's image on the shelf,
And seek within my inner self the God I often felt was near,
But in what image was not clear, I had no pre-conceived idea.

How does one find what one can't see, not easy for a man like me?
Who's used to seeing evidence to prove existence without doubt?
When it's a being never seen by mortals here upon this Earth with
No credentials to produce it has to be by faith alone we only know what he's about.

Evidence! Its well-known that it's not taken just on trust, to swear upon it is a must?
And who will be the judge of us to tell the truth upon 'the book'
Almighty God of course, dear me now I'm thinking blasphemy
But God forgives us all our sins if we confess them so I read,
So maybe in my hour of need I'll tell him all my doubts and if I'm good then just maybe,
He'll change them back to certainty.

David North

EVERY NIGHT AND DAY

Thoughts of you, I always invite,
With every single line I write,
My thinking never seems to stray,
I think about you night and day,
I wonder if we could ever be,
Together, forever, you and me,
You never notice I am there,
What can I do, to make you aware,
I wish you could see me, like I see you,
I wish you would want me, I really do,
My heart is broken, but you cannot see,
For I know that we, will never be,
Someday I may find someone like you,
But he will be second best, it's true,
Not to care for you, I should try,
But I fear I would rather die,
For my heart belongs to only you,
And no one else will ever do.

Susan Johnstone

COMMUNICATIONS

My son went to Holland and did very well
He fell for a Dutch girl, she's nice. I could tell
They now have two children; a girl and a boy
Adorable infants they bring me great joy
And now comes the sad bit – I love them so much
But I don't understand them – they speak double-Dutch
They know what I say, though they're both under seven
But they won't be taught English until they're eleven
I got me some books on English and Dutch
But I can't seem to grasp the grammar and such
But I'll keep on trying until I can speak
More than good morning and days of the week
Till the day that my Dutch is fit to be heard
I'm glad that my actions speak louder than words.

Dorothy Beaumont

FROM THE HEART

I'm nobody's girlfriend,
And nobody's wife,
How I wish I had someone,
In my life.

A nice, strong and good-looking man,
To hold me when he can.
To feel his warm embrace,
When I get colder.

A hug at the end of the day,
Round his shoulder,
Someone there to be mine,
Company, escort, a glass of wine.

My companion there for me,
It's got to really be,
So perfect, my man's a dish,
This is my only wish.

For him to come along,
I pray to god above,
To send me a man to love.

Caroline Janney

THE HEART SEES DEEPER THAN THE EYE

Predetermined in all things which have been witnessed with quiet composure
Heart memories, the recognition of each imperfection is stored away in a penitent's soul
The heart, the touchstone of man reveals undiscovered profiles of momentous scenarios
Each filed away like the fragrances the mind stores
Vast secrets are reclaimed and held in the hearts embrace
Each turbulent insight of life is consciously, securely recorded in preserved memory
So sacred inside the skeletal sculptured body
To which only God knows the secrets in our hearts
Such assurance gives tranquility to the mind
This acceptance is our only surety
What is witnessed however desolate, the heart's energy will never give it up
The evidence remains safe.

Hilary Jean Clark

I LOVE THE WAY YOU LOVE ME

I love the way you talk to me
I love the way you smile
I love that warming feeling
When you hold me for a while
I love you when you're angry
I love you when you're sad
I love you when you're happy
And I love you when you're bad
I love the way you hold my hand
I love the way you kiss me
I love the caring in your voice
When telling me you miss me
I love the way you make me mad
Your laughter when we disagree
I love you when you show concern
Not worried who may see
I love the things you say and do
Our love was meant to be
But most of all I love you
For the way that you love me.

Sue Brown

HOLY COMMUNION GIRL

She spread the silk across table and pinned it with bobby pins
till it was like a bat wing stunned with second hand needles.
It grew large in order to grow small and shaped
like a first communion dress dictated, white.

She slipped it over my eyes and my face till the silk was touching me;
outside it snows cherry blossom trees
I slide into a dream of cherry blossoms and pink snow
and I thought if I die before I am old I shall wear this dress.

She sews lace around my feet like spiderwebs hanging on.
I have done nothing wrong so I shall go to Heaven
I will swim at night
and swallow water made of beautiful things.

Fiona Donaghey

FIAT PANDA 1.1 ACTIVE ECO MANUAL

Another note from Stewart, what's he got to say?
'I saw this, mum, and thought of you, click on it today'
Fiat Panda, gleaming red, I'd better take a peek.
So now I have to tell you it was mine within a week.

Thirteen years have passed me by since last I had a drive,
I've bought myself a Highway Code, to conquer this I'll strive.
I do enjoy the freedom, just like I had before,
Nipping round from place to place, I couldn't ask for more.

I know I am an old 'un, but that's not how it feels,
Dragging round a shopping trolley? No, I've got my wheels.
No more climbing up the hills except when in the park,
Making sure where 'ere I go I'm home before it's dark.

Derbyshire Lane and Scarsdale, Bishops Court so steep,
Then there's Upper Albert Road, up Meadow Head I'll creep.
There's much more traffic on the roads, I know that I'll be steady,
With lots of lunatics around, for them I must be ready.

Now let's look on the bright side, I've got another chance.
Another pleasure to enjoy, now we no longer dance.
Alan's got his Scenic but he's fancying a Note.
Stewart's looking out for him and sending Dad a quote.

Will Dad buy another car? We'll have to wait and see,
He always takes a lot of time deciding, not like me.
Often when he does decide and then he find it's gone,
He'll walk away and mutter, there'll be another one.

Beryl Heathcote

OVERCOMING GRIEF

It happened about a month before
A hill I used to climb with my dad when I was four
I just don't know why I wanted to return
What this strange feeling was I just wanted to learn
So I started to climb up this jagged hill
Which always gave me an excitement and thrill
Struggling up the hill was murder
But I knew getting to the top wasn't much further
But as I reached the jagged peak I was in for a shock
For I met an old woman standing at the top and on a large rock
Why she was near the edge of the rock and on the hill I hadn't a clue
I thought it must have been for a view
But as I stopped and stared at her eyes
I could see she was in grief and couldn't hold back her outcries
So I asked what was wrong and why the pain
And then she started to explain
She said she was a widow and had one child only
But now she feels oh so very lonely
'Because my child had recently died,' she sighed
and said, that she'd only known him for nineteen years
as she wiped her eyes of her tears
and explained she had nothing left to live for
and so wanted to die for she couldn't take anymore
so she started to climb the ledge
right up to the edge
and so the old lady jumped off the hill, claiming it was her calling
but I'm glad I caught her by her hand while she was falling
and so I pulled her up with all my might
for I didn't want her to die without putting up a fight
so overcoming the shock of what just happened, I started to explain
that there was a way of overcoming her grief and pain
for by worshipping God with faith you must
and be earning His trust
god will help you with your pain
and to see your child alive again
for to God a child's just asleep not dead
and can be brought back to life and awakened as if in a bed
for now the old lady is not in so much grief
because my words gave her some comfort and relief
for God will soon resurrect all the dead
for this is something He's promised and said.

Donato Genchi

ROCK 'A' BILLY VAMPIRE

Pulling up at the dance hall
The joint was jumping,
Hep-cats were a'bopping
Bourbon shots and scrumpy flowing
The floor was awash with boozed fights – a'blazing.

I sort my prey a guy comes into view
Wrecking his best to the beat of rock and roll
I could tell his chick was heading for a rumble
I knew she couldn't win, to my charming ways.

The night wore on and the chicky run was on the cards
He was the prize the cars sped along the cliff road,
My vision blurred with drink,

She drove a Ford V8 hotrod and I a '59 Cadillac hearse,
It was agreed the winner got the guy,
I would have them both, Fatale Femme Vampire
Off with smoking tyres, wheels burning
The cliff edge closed, neither was giving an inch,
Air borne I jumped and caught her jugular as we fell,
Drinking sweet adrenaline rich nectar
I let her go drained of blood, and flew on the wing
As the cars plummeted I caught the cliff near the top,

A crowd gathered to the spectacle of cars
Triumphant impact on the beach below
Climbing down he was mine Andy
What guts you've got chick Varrena, spirit
None I said as I drank and then fed him from the blood of my wrist,
We are one Immortal Rockabillies,
I said together for eternity.

Cheers arose as we emerged at the cliff edge, the party's just starting.

Kevin Clemo

ESPECIALLY FOR YOU

In the arms of an angel
I rest my weary wing
When I am tired
I hear my brother sing
He is a family angel
With our other kins
In the arms of an angel
My brother Syl

In the arms of an angel
My sister Ionie
She had a golden heart
And spirits that live
In the arms of an angel
I rest my weary wing
In the arms of an angel
My sister Ionie

Our brother Syl
Our sister Ionie
Was unique and free
They had spirits that the world could see
For they were forever full of glee
In the arms of an angel
Our brother Syl
In the arms of an angel
Our sister Ionie

I know that they are happy
For when the sun shines on me
I feel a special glow
And I know
That it's my sister Ionie
And my brother Syl

In the arms of an angel
Our brother Syl
In the arms of an angel
Our sister Ionie

I'll say hip hip hooray
For Ionie Cole Lenoard
I'll say hip, hip hooray
For Sylvanous Nathaniel Cole
For they lived and they died
And now they are free

In the arms of an angel
Our sister Ionie
In the arms of an angel
Our brother Syl.

Carolie Cole Pemberton

SHAKESPEARE

Didst though repeat what I just said?
Whilst I am known to quit all jest
You played into my rightful request,
By alas repeating what I just said,
Conversation with classic lore
Shakespeare aimed to the core
Medieval tones he scored,
Forthright and forthwith
With words theatrically deplored
Love and life stored,
Creating poems and sonnets
Hitherto reading
Historical plays staged
For historians to praise,
Whilst William Shakespeare
Went his way yielding
Quoting a self-indulgent system
Thereafter historic commodity poised
Controlled lyrics and voice,
The great Bard of Avon and Ware
William Shakespeare 1564 – 1660.

Barbara R Lockwood

A MIRACLE NO MORE

When I sit back and look
Over our time,
I used to smile and laugh,
Now I only cry.

We had a future,
We had our plans,
A promise to always
Walk hand-in-hand.

We were together,
We were a team,
We were in love,
So it seemed.

You made me happy,
You gave me hope,
You gave me life,
I have never known.

You made a promise,
Then took it back,
Taking away
The only love I ever had.

You made me feel worthy,
Like I was the only one,
But you drifted away,
Leaving me alone.

You said you pretended,
About the way you feel,
Leaving me with nothing,
My heart yet to heal.

Now I feel empty,
Like nothing is real,
My passions have perished,
My heart will not heal.

But life goes on,
So what they say,
But all I feel,
Is misery and pain.

You have destroyed who I am,
Taken away my life,
My passions, my enjoyments,
My future no longer bright.

Now I must live,
In a world without hope,
In a world without love,
In a world without me.

But I will try to heal,
Though my wounds are still sore,
Because you are only a memory,
A miracle no more.

Claire Jones

THE HOUSE NEXT DOOR

Diana and Brian had been thro' a sticky patch,
They wanted to get away,
A friend had a house to let in the sticks,
So they moved in right away.

Life was peaceful there at first,
Then Diana began to hear noises nearby,
A couples discordant voices from next door,
Shirley found herself wondering why.

One evening, while she was in the kitchen,
From over the wall came a woman's scream,
This was followed by a muffled gasp,
It's happening again, she thought, *like a bad dream!*

Brian reluctantly agreed to go next door,
Diana waited, filled with dismay,
When he returned he said no one was there,
'You must have imagined it!' he cried – and turned away.

Things were not the same after that,
Brian was out on business one night,
Diana went upstairs to get ready for bed,
Suddenly, from the empty house, came a light.

This time the couple were at their window,
The woman lay on the floor, the man as if turned to stone,
He lifted her body, turned her face towards Diana,
Petrified, the girl saw the features were *her own*.

Ann J Furley

POETIC JUSTICE

'Coffee, Prime Minister? Good trip to the Middle East?'

'That would be nice.
And James, fetch some champagne to put on ice.
I've helped our friends and saved some jobs.
It's nice to thwart those peacenik yobs.'

'Shall I arrange a press release?'

'Yes, tell my scribe to spin a piece
And make quite sure he scores a goal
With details of my leading role.'

'It does sound sinister.
I suppose you know best Prime Minister.
But was it right to grease some palms
To get those orders for our arms.
Rowan Williams might foil your plan with his theocracy
When he finds you weren't supporting democracy.'

'James, please bear in mind that telling lies
Is just the art of compromise.'

'I'm sorry, but don't you think it seems
Unwise to sell our arms to such regimes?
Look at the problems caused by Bush. He thought the world was just a garden
Where he could play war games with Bin Laden.
Now our soldiers get the flak.
I'm sure they feel shot in the back.
They're flown in daily packed in boxes.
I wish instead they were apples; perhaps Coxes.
Not much to be proud of for the boffins
Designing ways to fill up coffins,
And parents grieving at the funeral parade
Not knowing where the guilty guns were made.'

'Oh do shut up, James. I have a job to do.
So do you.
I hear your voice but there's no choice.
Our workers make our guns and planes
In times of loss and times of gains.
When there's a war it brings them joy
Knowing they're safe in our employ.
What's the matter? You've been a bore
Since you opened the door.'

'I am feeling sad I must confess.
I wanted just to understand, nothing more, nothing less.

I see now that Hugh was just a toy.
But to me he was a joy, just a boy.
Now he's dead, not home on leave,
And I'm still learning how to grieve.'

'What are you saying, James? Have I gone barmy?
Your son was in the army?'

'Afghanistan. Perhaps you read the casualty statistics
Just to keep up with your arms ballistics!
They found this shrapnel in his head.
It's why he's dead.'

James put the twisted metal on the table.
'Made in Derby' said its label.

'I have no life now, Sir, no real motives.
I was never one for lighting votives.
I've paid the price and you must too.
This place is rotten through and through.'

He drew a weapon from his coat
And aimed it at his victim's throat.

'Please James, let's sit and talk.
The sun is out. Let's take a walk.'

'Too late Sir, now!
Just time for you to take your bow.
But rest assured you're not alone.
In God's good time we'll all atone.
There is a twist that you should hear
Before you shed your final tear.
Bahrein is where I bought this pistol.
But it says just here it was made in Bristol.'
James shot his master in the chest. The stricken man just sank.
His last thought was, *it's just a prank*.
He didn't hear the second shot. The same gun.
Now two persons' blood pooled into one.

The cover-up was all efficiency.
Number 10 showed no deficiency.
The papers said how very sad;
The secretary was never bad,
Just overcome with grief and loss.
He went insane and shot his boss.
But James had known how lies would spread
And used his head.
Too late they searched his clothes and found a pocket full of pens
With one drilled out to hide a lens.

What made the Party much more bitter
Was to find concealed a small transmitter.

When Channel 4 broadcast the story
James was revered and cast in glory.
Thousands resigned their jobs in Defence.
It made more sense than deference.
There was no way to change the past
But consciences bore fruit at last.

Great changes came and Parties fought
For favours bought.
More games, old aims dressed up as new.
A pious leader praying in his pew
God competing with his derision
For James, the architect of a naïve and sentimental decision.
There were more subtle ways to become ascendant.
A republic will need a president.

Mike Joslin

AN AFTERNOON WELL SPENT

I called in at the garden centre just the other day
I only stopped to look around and pass an hour away
Oh the glory of the colours, the blues, the reds, the greens
It filled my eyes with wonder, the best I have ever seen
So though I only stopped to have a browse
I've checked up on my 'lolly,' I find I'm not completely broke
So I run to get a trolley, there's holly hocks, forget-me-nots
All tempting me to buy take care you do not overspend
I promise I will try, Antirrhinum's, Aquilegia I will buy a box of each
I have moved on to the roses, now I'm looking for a peach
Delphinium, dianthus, I will buy a few of those
I must move on, control myself or I will buy another rose
Geranium, godetia they all appeal to me
I must take care, or once again, I'll buy everything I see
I will make my way to checkout now
It's been a frantic dash
I will unload my trolley and hope I have the cash!

R Giddings

THE PLYMOUTH BLITZ

The Phoney War was over and the bombs began to fall,
The sight from not too far away, was of one great fireball;
The might of Nazi airpower which continued through the night.
Made sure that in the morning the whole place was alight;
The sound of bombs exploding, mixed with gunfire far and near,
Made us all a little nervy, 'The real word was fear,'
The early morning after was a sight of real disaster,
There were bodies mixed with debris in the streets,
The Nazis were still winning, this was only the beginning,
It was yet another one of those defeats.
Our Fathers were away, so each and every day our Mothers had to plan the week ahead,
There wasn't much to choose from, and there wasn't much of that,
But come what may the kids were always fed.
As children we were plucky, and more than often lucky,
We would lie and watch the dogfight in the sky,
These battles were amusing, and a little bit confusing,
We didn't know that one of them would die.
As children of the thirties, things that constituted 'dirties'
Was to run away when someone said, 'You're dead,'
If you didn't play the game, you could never play again,
So you just ran home to Mum and straight to bed.
Our shelter was our second home, our pets would also stay,
At times we'd have a body count and find ourselves a stray,
We never really slept a lot, all we really did was doze,
It was dreadful in the winter when the water level rose.
Taking turns to pump we would try to keep it dry,
But in the summer it was different, we would simply lie and fry.
Those months of war soon took their toll, of body, spirit and sometimes soul.
Things got better, as they always do,
The improvement began in forty two,
At last it seemed we were winning the war,
The news was good, but our backs were sore;
Back to our beds, from that hole in the ground,
Even our toys were easily found;
Those months in the past we shall never forget,
And the childhood we lost, we lost regret.

Mr Gordon Ramsey

A CHILD'S WARTIME MEMORY

In was nineteen thirty-nine, when we children of that era
Found our lives were about to change,
How well do I remember,
From that time in September
How things were to seem so very strange.

All the hustle and the bustle
As the grown-ups came to tussle
With the rationing of clothing and provisions,
Tearfully parting from their men
Not knowing if they'd ever meet again.
The coming years would be making those decisions.

The fear from the above, reigned terror down below
As people lay sleeping in their bed,
Causing death and destruction
Without any compunction
Not caring where it all led.

At last the moment came
When this treacherous war game
Came to its final conclusion
Leaving memories of sadness
From the dreaded days of madness
Life as we used to know it
Can never be the same.

Leslie Frank Checkley

MOONLIGHT

My darling I see you outside by the pond
Someone I am very fond
Looking across the black water
Some moonlight hits the ripples
I walk towards you putting my hand around you tight
You turn to me in fright
I see your beautiful face
What I see the moonlight race.

Moonlight shining so bright, at night you get a fright
My darling's name is Lizzy, her hair not as frizzy
Your heart beats fast like a fast moving train, we look up and it starts to rain.

Kaela Khaine

ZORRO

It is the first lie I remember.
The comic I borrowed from Dunny up the road
Was glossier than the Dandy and far more realistic.
It had Zorro.
What kind of name was that?
He didn't shoot arrows, didn't sink e-boats.
He was the opposite of Anglo-Saxon,
He was chic.
The artwork was darkly foreboding
And the bubbles were full of bold declarations.
There was more to this than Beryl the Peril.
Was it some devil-may-care zeitgeist or pure chance
That made Mrs Pordess get a Zorro outfit in stock?
It dangled between the hula-hoops and Lone Star six-shooters
With packaging as portentous as the comic –
Vivid black and red.
Inside there was a round boot polish hat,
A plastic touche sword, a plastic cape,
Some stripes you stick down the side of your trousers.
I'd only gone there for caps.

Mrs Pordess was a friend of the family.
In our small village every occupant of every house knew everyone else's back story.
Genealogy followed you around and bore down on bad behaviour.

'My gran's just on her way,' I said.
'She knows about Zorro she . . . took us to the Odeon . . .
She said I could pick up that set in the window . . . to make sure I got one . . . '
A liver-spotted hand passed it over the counter,
Over the Spitfires and Match-box vans.
'She won't be long,' I said and slinked to the door.
Rows of knowing dolls looked down in horror.
I scarpered to the top of Moorfields,
Clawed the cellophane off with a thumbnail,
Pressed out the hat, tied on the cape, fitted the tip on the sword, unravelled the taper.

That wasn't me darting behind bungalows and into the field.
That was Zorro – fencing with his conscience.

Peter Ardern

LOVE

Love is worth saving I think you should know
But if we never fall in love then how can we grow
How can an hour feel like a day?
When the person you love is so far away
When you hope that that person feels the same too
That that person is sitting there thinking the same about you
That it'll all be alright you'll see in the end
That love is worth sharing and to us it will send
A message of hope that will see our way through
But after all's said and one, we know what to do
We take it and hold it and make it grow strong
And keep it together so it never goes wrong
We think of the days when we laugh and hold hands
And think of the love that is cleansing our lands
Think of the times when you're bursting with joy
You feel like a child with their first Christmas toy
You think of the time that's coming our way
And hoping that love is coming to stay
But we've been there 'n' done that and let's not pretend
That love is our saviour, our guidance, our friend
Love can be rotten and hurtful and cruel
So when it raises its head, you know it's a duel
But you have to sit back and let it fit like a glove
Open the door and welcome in love.
Please.

Paul M Clarkson

BLACKBURN, LANCASHIRE

The big dray horses pulling barrels of Thwaites to the
Brewery were still working here on a recent visit to Blackburn.
I climbed to the roof top parking over the shopping centre
Motoring under the Max Headroom signs.
I left the car and walked around the rooftops,
The town coming into view around every turn.

The town looked much smaller than when I last visited it
In 1957 at the age of twelve
The greenbelt had recently expanded, now green open valleys
Rolling into the distant Lancashire countryside where once
There was nothing but mill factories and smoking factory chimneys.
Then I remembered walking across a big town square to the main
Northern route out of town roughly in the direction I was gazing now

A strangely empty landscape now, but then just a mass of mill
Factories all bleak, black and hazy through the smoke.
The town square is also gone, leaving a modern roof-parking
Shopping mall. I took the lift down to the ground floor.
It seemed to be working, had tea at a tea room hearing the clip-clop of the brewery wagon
As the horse carts came passing by,
The towns only concession to the past.
Now all gone but I am glad I made the journey for I had caught a glimpse of the last days of King Cotton
At work and know that was completely different world than the one we see now,
But it did make me wonder about what people are doing now with their lives.

Without their factories.
For a moment I took a glimpse of another age, the age of King Cotton,
It's no longer here.
The town seemed healthier and now you could see far into the distance from the rooftops.
It even managed to look a little prosperous, but not for me, the temperance movement
looked as though it had passed the town goodbye.
Just another hole to fill the Albert Hall.

Philip John Loudon

SUPERSTAR

I don't want to be a star on the stage
That was never meant for me
But a real star
Is what I want to be
So fly me to the sky
Let me be among real stars
Amidst all the greatest
And be near Jupiter and Mars
And if you should be looking up
You will know which one is me
I shall be the biggest
And the brightest star you see
So this is my destiny
To be a real star for evermore
A very special superstar
Like there has never been before
I did not want to be a star on the stage
And you may wonder why
But I arose to stardom
When I came to the sky.

Joan Herniman

CLUMSY!

Watch me fall,
Watch me crawl,
Watch me, 'cause,
I am standing tall.

There is love,
I have on my mind,
This love it makes me,
Feel so fine.

I would love to see,
This love most days,
It's a love that cannot be replaced,
This love I would sit on my lap,
It would be forever and that is a fact.

I'm not sure if my love has a clue,
Cos it's a love that's well over due,
And now, the answer has been found,
My love has turned my life around.

I'm glad I found him, I'm glad he found me,
I'm glad he satisfied all my needs,
This is a love it will forever be seen,
My love his name is Mr Green.

Yvette Avonda Rose

THE GIFT OF TIME

The air today was crisp clear, but very cold,
As we set off heading for Eastbourne's promenade to behold,
We sampled hot chocolate, in the Wish Tower café,
To warm us on this very winter's day.

From the Wish Tower we walked towards Holywell,
The wind biting, and chilling, creating its spell,
Silver Dale walk, we decided to climb to a higher stage.
Following the path towards the car, and soon engage.

We drove towards Beachy Head, along the ridge,
Admiring the scenery, far more than just average,
Clear was the view which encountered our vision,
The glorious downs with its undulating mission,

Motoring down to the Cuckmere, the meandering river,
Winding its way so lazily, shining like silver,
Up the hill to Seaford, a busy seaside town,
Where houses shone like mirages. A useful pronoun.

Down the hill from Seaford, the downs were majestically real,
Stretching and reaching, mystical, the atmosphere ideal.
Reaching Alfriston the village of surreal wonder,
Very sleepy but yet held a captivating lustre.

Passing DRUSILLA'S, where all seemed at rest,
Animals tucked up warm and cosy free from stress.
Waiting for a train to pass over the level crossing,
Berwick has a charm, if only a spot of train spotting.

Passing the reservoir where the chilly wind still blew,
Visibility was restricted, hedges were difficult to peep through.
Travelling onto St Bede's its here where we turn right,
Passing Michelham priory historic in value, an awesome sight.

Close to Arlington race track where all is closed at present,
A popular venue for every age, and competitive contestant,
So to the dual carriageway, the A twenty-two,
Bringing us back to Hailsham town, which we drove through,

This morning although extremely cold and windy,
Minus one at times, said the thermometers registering committee
The views across the Sussex downs and out to sea,
Were quite phenomenal, an awe-inspiring moment of creativity.

Lorna Tippett

Thank you Janet, Love Lorna

THE SILENT SCREAMS WITHIN

Tortuous, twisted, trembling, and terrified
This innocent mind, mutilated, and contorted, to its depths
Along with massive invisible bruises, deep scars, and a longing to be healed
The enormity of such a tortuous burden, lays heavy within
Like granite in juxtaposition, with life's constant tormented moments, cemented between
Adversity, anger, and annihilation, are always a constant presence within this life
These torments remain the intentions of the evil perpetrator
The heart, repeatedly ripped apart, by such evil 'persona non grata'
The devastating pain remains, and ripples throughout a fragile frame
Lingering, lasting, load, lays heavy within, even into adulthood
Only prayers, along with a miracle, would be a release for this innocence
The crippling mental torture by a gargantuan presence, remains constant
Unceasing, is the tormentor, in the acts of demonstrative, evil, abuse
All avenues of escape, seemed insurmountable, throughout life
Only the victim's silent screams, echoed far, into the universe, and beyond
Will this evil torment ever cease, was the prayer from a life so fragile
Only as the tortuous years passed, was there hope for a glimmer of light on the horizon
The young child grew into an adult, and prayed fervently for closure of this crippling torment
If only the perpetrator could be removed from its prominent position in their life
Then suddenly, the terrible twisted thorn, which pierced the side of the child. Died!
This evil of emotional abuse, at last, lay within the Earth's crust
Seeping its gargantuan evil abusive powers into the unforgiving cold, damp, dark earth
Now the relieved child and adult 'rejoiced,' their heart and emotions lifted forever
The child cried visibly, and screamed silently for joy, at the demise of this evil perpetrator
All those very long, tortuous years of abuse, have left a heavy burden, of emotional scars
The adult can now pray for inner healing, the lifting of the load, and life of happiness
Even now, the child and adult, still visibly show the emotion of the silent screams within!

Nigel Lloyd Maltby

THIS BEAUTIFUL LAND

To see the beautiful red sunset that covers a silent dale
Their wild beauty is so outstanding in the land of Wales
Those deep valleys where the beauty stands out so proud
The meadows, the lush green grass and the heather covers the high grounds

When the winter snow comes it spreads across the hills in a white snow cap
The mountaineers scales those mountains with guide and large printed map
There are days when the fields and hills are covered in their cloaks of mist
That hard freezing weather now holds the mountains and dales in its fist

The mountain screams have not begone a large sea of snow and ice
The farmyard is cut off the farmer ploughs his way thro' this wall of ice
Then he gathers his sheep and cows and takes them to their pens and barns
Where those large drifts of snow can't do anymore because they free from harm

Then the spring arrives those tiny snowdrops are now covering the open ground
The new life begins the farmer take his sheep to the upper ground
Then the countryside smiles the forest comes alive and becomes green again
Those spring clouds they water the dales and hills with gentle rain

To watch the beautiful sunrise now brings warmth and sunshine to the dales
I love to walk thro' the fields and see the beauty of Wales
Then the apple blossom dresses those orchard apples and pear trees
Where you smell the sweet air and the white clouds run so free.

John F Grainger

SICKNESS

Sickness, unwelcome caller to my door,
Your trunk and case across my threshold force.
These limbs, once chimed with vigour, dampened at source;
This hacking, lung-pit vileness drenched with fever.
My medication punctuates each hour
And torpid, this page with words I splutter;
To feel each cough mock my sculpted meter;
With focus waning, metaphors turn sour.
My betters crafted worlds from their sick beds:
Stevenson, Keats breathed imagination isles
Of rare treasure, or let fly nightingales,
Borne up, to soar on air from tired lungs.
If I could work small billows to my mind,
Like these, to fire dross to something refined!

Anthony John Webster

DIAMOND JUBILEE OF HER MAJESTY THE QUEEN

Your Majesty Noble Queen so great, so dear,
We are delighted to wish you happiness and good cheer,
I write joyful lines on your sixty year reign so fine,
A beloved Queen who is good and very kind,
Your Majesty has given unwavering service to all,
You bring pleasure and happiness to big and small,
We are full of praise of your sixty year reign,
People are happy to see you again and again,
Subjects of your realm so far and wide,
Await your arrival with great joy and pride,
It is wonderful to see how you rule with such grace,
Makes us all carry smiles of happiness on each face,
You work with care to bring contentment to everyone,
We are proud of you for all the good you have done,
We wish you many happy years to abide,
It's the wish of the people in the world that's wide,
For your Diamond Jubilee we send many good wishes your way,
We wish you good health and happiness every single day.

Kamala Dias

SWAN

They hang out, scared to be alone.
Thick U bend pipes. Their hissy wings explode,
Snowy as bath bombs in a don't-care-a-jot
Whity supremacy stretch. There's such a lot
Of 'swan' stuff: affairs with humans, swan songs,
Ballet, matches, dressing up as gods
And really they're just an excuse to ride
Along and buy ice creams at our lakeside,
Get rid of mouldy bread, amuse the kids,
Skim stones and scatter litter in the bins
Pamper those false monogamists, smug
Orange beaked, knob-headed, black-eyed thugs.
Bring back the carmina burana days,
Roast swan, black on a spit, fat on a plate
While I, this ugly duckling, speckled brown,
Cartooned by quacks from tinsel town
Paddle with my mates, waddle with my drake,
Remind those pound signs we too own this lake.

Helen Kay

COSMOS

The rotating galaxies, spiral, elliptical
the Milky Way a giant kaleidoscopic Catherine wheel
a Galactic Halo, containing clusters of timeworn stars
crumbling, jaded

this agglomerate universe
a continuous creation of matter
an immense atom

I imagine floating in space's infinity
through the nomadic unsettled orbits of
the moving celestial spheres

far in the distance
a luminescent Quasar, appears
far flung to the edge of the universe
it shudders
displaying a vermilion mass
of haunting spectral lines

I watch in silent awe
as the giant nova catastrophically collapses inwards
into a membrane of blackness

in unison, the eclipsing binary duet sing
orienteering and clanging slowly,
the brilliance of the stinging scorpius
striking

I freefall
and land on the albite moon
where the dark denticulate mountains
shadow the depressions of the polygonal Maria

I feel
its gravitational stimulus
tugging at the tide of Syzygy . . .

Zabine Mirza

THE DAY THE LOVE DIED

He took my love on Monday
And with it my hope died
Crying
It's not Sunday
Limbs leaden,
Back broken heart's tired

He took my love on Monday
Sickness welling up
Inside
Washing linens
Scrubbing skin
Putrid stench along my thighs

He took my love on Monday
Embarrassed
Undignified
Only sis the ear,
My sanity
As blind, I trudge this murky mire

He took my love on Monday
My heart seared
And scorched
With fire
Stifled voice, lips crack
Eyes afraid and wild

He took my love on Monday
And demons walked right in
A winter's passed
It's Sunday Spring
So why am I still . . .
Crying?

Pauline Tomlin

NO FINER LEGACY

Travelling along life's highway,
With all its up and downs –
Not knowing what the future may hold –
Can be very daunting.
But isn't it what we do with our lives that matter?
The people we meet, the friends we make and keep.
How we cope with adversity and the successes we notch up.

Encouragement leaves such memories that cannot be erased.
Legacies come in many forms,
Not just in monetary terms.
To be missed and leave a lot of love behind,
Is one of life's successes.
And if, having made our mark in some field of achievement,
Be is spiritually, physically, or in the arts –
Then we were surely blessed
And the world will know.

From disadvantaged
Beginnings and times of strife –
It is not how we started in life –
Though humble it may have been –
But how we finish that counts.
There is no finer legacy . . .

Agnes Berry

SLAM TENNIS

It's August, start of the tennis fortnight
Tim Henman, Andy Murray in the spotlight
Both are trying to be number one
But a couple of slams and they're gone
Every August they have a bash
To win the title and the cash
But it's always someone else to win
Wow what a tournament they've been in
Neither have the power or the will
But there's many a follower on Henman's hill.

Dawn Moore

BREAD AND BUTTER DAYS

When we were young
We'd go to the flicks
Stuff our face with lollipops
Crisps and lick – or – riss

We'd dance by the juke box
Fish by the pier
We'd sit by the lamppost
Till the night-time drew near
And we'd laugh, telling tales of what had gone on
Between Mathew and Susan, Peter and John
No drugs, no drug dealers, we could sleep in our beds
We could walk twice the mile, without lead in our heads

Our bread and butter days, had no discontent
They had a God at the beginning and a Jesus
At the end, and never we feared that we'd fail the rent
Or live on the streets, or live in a tent
Or how high the price we'd have to pay
From the start to the finish, or the end of our day

You could knock on the door for a cup of sugar or two
And sit down for ages without hardly a sound
Excepting for bees, as they droned all around
No screaming or revving motorbikes whizzing by
No tin cans of beer on the walls where birds fly
You could walk down the lane, every face you could greet
You could stand on the pavement – without shit on your feet
And for all of the worries you had come by that day
There was always someone to listen, while you had your say

When we were young, we'd go to the flicks
Stuff our faces with lollipops, crisps and
Lick-or-riss.

Diana Mullin

RAISING THE STANDARD

In this year of 2012 we celebrate
The Diamond Jubilee of HM Elizabeth II
The Olympic banner too will wave
High, fast and strong to the people beckon
Oh, what joy to run to jump or swim
In London's 2012 Olympic Games
A fluttering of athletes nimble and light of limb
Lepidoptera drawn to the eternal flame.

In my plimsoll days
The school gym was not for me
From parallel bars and french chalky swings
I fled with alacrity
The playing field too was risky
Dodging the hockey stick's clattering threat
The 'bully off' I quickly acknowledged
Was a jolly that commanded respect
So I'll excuse myself from the Olympics
As a spectator drybob wet
Horrors of past sports days is
A cautionary tale for one so athletically inept
If I were to catch the feverish endeavour
Of a pow-wow of commentators oozing P. Bees
An over the top marathon
Would freeze my faculties
Oh the hype of it
Oh the gripe of it – arrest the T.V
The dizzying busy-ing height of it
Plays not a fanfare for me.

Lucy Green

POEM FOR TODAY

I wrote a poem yesterday, that didn't make much sense,
I shall revise it now and see, it's in the present tense!
To make a poem logical, it surely must ensure,
That what it does insinuate, is something true and pure!

It must not be ridiculous, or something quite insane!
But verse quite understandable, that brings no mental pain;
Initially, its title should, alert some interest keen;
Which brings intrigue and mystery, that might remain unseen!

A thing which makes the reader want, to study, for some clue,
While hoping that the writer will, in time – bring in a few!
Those who peruse such narrative, must scan with lots of hope;
The writer too, should also try, to introduce must scope!

In writing such a brilliant ode, the poet should apply,
A good degree of rhyming words, and rhythm worth a try!
Descriptions formed, should smoothly glide and also gently flow;
In ways which readers understand – and recognising, know!

My vain attempt of yesterday, to entertain in rhyme,
Today's result may bear success, when read in altered time!
Mistakes once made – and now undone,
Tomorrow's epic, could yet – become!

Ron Bissett

DESPAIR

Her heart, like her head was hung low. Held there by the burdens of her life,
All those heavy pains and all the strife were heaped upon her blow by blow.
Demented sirens kept her from rest and maintained a fragile mind at best.
The fevered tumult in her sinewy arms caused her to flinch and scowl to rise,
And show the terrors of her torn psyche in her cold and oft' tormented eyes.

There was no joy in life, no hope filled straw her shaking fingers might grasp.
As the last tears now lay dry upon the pallid skinned face once bathed in light,
But no more, no more cherished clasp, or look of warmth from passing fan.
The age of wonder is now gone, like the last light of a distant dying star and,
In its place there remains only forlorn hope and any future gripped in fright,
Until, at last she finds peace which awaits her now in deaths endless night.

Do not look unkindly on her ravaged face, or show disgust or cruel glance.
What lies here before you now was once held beauteous and sought by all,
And those same admirers saw her fall, and stood aside as fate and decreed,
Lest her sickness tarnish with her touch, or any kindness ask too much.
Lay her gently in the folds of her final sleep, and wrap her warmly in her silk,
Close her wounded eyes that none might see her in her panic and in her pain,
And if God there be then on some distant shore may her beauty rise again.

Colin Curtis

CHILDREN OF THE APOCALYPSE

Children of the Apocalypse – please know my fears,
As we approach the next ten thousand years.
If you wish to possess a future.
If this planet is to survive.
You must consider your present.
Or
There will be no one to hear
The wind in the trees, the crash of the waves.

There will be no one to smell
The scent of a rose, new mown hay.

There will no one to taste
The salt on their lover's cheek.

There will no one to dream, to think , scheme.
There will be no one to sense
The atmosphere of love at first sight.

There will be no one to feel the soft skin of a newborn baby.
There will be no one to feel the need to procreate.
There will be one to feel.
There will be no one.
There will be
The end.

Stu Phillips

RECONCILIATION

(Prompted by the Truth & Reconciliation Commission in South Africa)

Far apart, far apart,
Sundered by a monstrous act.
Venomed splinter in the heart –
Useless to deny the fact.
But the poison's active still;
Hard to bear, the nagging pain –
Hard to think peace ever will
Invade and soothe the heart again.

Far apart, far apart.
How could I be half so vile?
How can I relieve the smart?
Surely not by bland denial.
Mirrored in my conscience now
I must bear it face to face –
Know myself and so avow
The fact of my deserved disgrace.

This painful truth must surely reinforce
The will to try and share my victim's pain
And so to know the horrors of remorse.
A futile gesture? Suffering in vain?
But if that sterile wish could lead me on
To piercing sorrow, making me decide
To seek for pardon from the injured one
And so to crush all vestiges of pride . . .

. . . then surely only that can set me free
Although the pain might dog me to the grave.
Could such a gesture also be the key
To bring release to such a one, and pave
The way to break the tyranny of hate,
Allowing him to dissipate his pain
Not letting it forever dominate
His life, but freeing him to live again?

I can beg that God may hear my prayer
And help him in that bitterest of hurt,
So leading to those healing waters where
Forgiveness is enabled to convert
The poison I injected in his soul
To nourishment whose action will sustain
And make his liberated spirit whole,
So opening up the path to life again.

Dare I hope? Dare I hope?
If I ask his pardon now
May there still remain some scope
For forgiveness yet to flower?
Can such blessed healing come
To repair such devastation,
Wakening love and bringing some
Chance of reconciliation?

Mr Vaughan Stone

LOWESTOFT HUMAN JETSAM

The Suffolk town of Lowestoft
Made famous the land throughout
By the once great fishing industry
And the herring for who keen eyes would scout
The men who crewed the fishing boats
Hard and intrepid as men could be
Fought hard to feed the nation
With the fruits of the North Sea

With the tides the boats would sail
Womenfolk waving their sad goodbye
Returning home to sit and pray
Their men working that hell would not die
Through raging storms the men searched wide
Icy waters chilling them to the bone
Praying for a fruitful catch
And an early return to the warmth of home

Sadly now those days are gone
Replaced by the oilfield industry
But still you'll see him as you walk the coast
With his aching eyes scouring the sea
The fishermen now beached and done
Ancient skill required no more
In his eyes worth is less than that
Of the jetsam that litters the shore.

Don Woods

WITHIN AN ENGLISH WOOD

Let me lie and sleep 'The Sleep'
Where memories and dreams do keep,
Blesséd and curséd both the same
Free from sorrow. Free from pain.

Allow me rest 'neath the broad-leaved trees,
Far from well-trodden paths will please.
Beneath the spread of the powerful Elm,
And the mighty Oak, king of woodland realm.

Beneath the Beach, the Ash and Lime,
The Willow, Alder: Rest sublime.
What mortal soul could wish for more,
Rest 'neath the Walnut, Sycamore.

And gazing up at summer sky,
On mossy blanket where I lie,
The Maple giving shade to see
The flowering Wood Anemone.

The Stitchwort and the Daffodil,
Birds nest Orchid gives a thrill.
Sweet Violet and so much more
To grace my special forest floor.

'Midst the Bluebells and the' Foxglove
In the clearings that I love,
Where as a child I often stood
Within an ancient English wood.

So scatter me 'neath the canopies
Of England's finest woodland trees,
Where childhood days spent so carefree,
I chose to roam so thankfully.

Jim Ryder

VALUES

Some people get their priorities wrong,
They don't look around them as life rushes on.
Their days are spent in a mad endless rush,
Jostling each other as they fight through the crush.
Hooting and fumes from cars in long rows,
Can bring on a headache as everyone knows!
Some people possess a remarkable brain,
And climb up the ladder of fortune and fame.
Their greatest objective is piling up money,
They don't even notice if it's cloudy or sunny.
Weekend in front of the TV they spend,
A wood and glass idol on which they depend,
Occasionally rising to pour out a drink,
Until they are staggering around on the brink!
A sherry, a brandy, or sometimes a whisky,
Till everything goes and they start to feel frisky!
They suddenly realise that life's passed them by.
'It's time I retired' is the usual cry.
They come down to Earth with a bump. . . . They are old,
Life hangs on a thread and it's worth more than gold.
The best things in this life are the things that are free,
You don't pay a penny, but just look and see.
A beautiful sunset spread out in the sky,
It's breathtaking beauty could just make you cry.
It's reflection on water, so silent and still,
When its last rays are touching a far distant hill.
A pinewood in winter, its trees tipped with snow,
The snow through the branches making them glow.
A walk by the shore with the wind in the waves,
The song of the sea upon rocks and in caves.
The twitter of swallows as they dart through the air,
Dipping and diving with never a care . . .
And the moon and the stars on a clear frosty night.
The love of a dear one, the kiss of a child,
Clouds in a storm when they're wind-tossed and wild.
These are the values I would put first,
Other people can wine and dine till they burst . . .
They can keep their diamonds and all their fast cars,
They can charter a spaceship and take off for Mars!
Their mansions, their riches mean nothing to me . . .
The best things in life are the things which are free . . .

Liz Osmond

BISCUIT TINS

Grandma had a biscuit tin
Old and round, colours worn thin,
Inside were treasures from long ago,
When much younger she used to sew,
There were buckles and buttons by the score,
I played with them on the floor,

Brass studs from coats and sleeves,
Wooden shapes with painted leaves,
Tiny ones from baby clothes,
Black and navy – lots of those,
Pretty glass, pearlies too,
Fancy shapes a delicate hue,
I like the buckles too –
Bold and shiny – still looked new,
Soldiers' buckles had a crest,
But nurses were the best,
Small ones were neat and square,
The blue buckles were a pair,

All the buttons and buckles
Told a story,
Once when new were in their glory,
Grandma's old biscuit tin,
Really did have treasures in!

Sheila Waller

'DEMONSIDE' BUS 666 STAND 2L

Take this bus to Demon land
It's not far from here.
Climb aboard and pay your fare
No time for you to spare.

Behind his wheel the driver sits
His glare will shake your bones.
Break the cobwebs, climb the stairs
Feel the damp and chilling air.

Reserved for you a window seat
Watch your life go by.
Read the road signs as you pass
They'll only make you cry.

Passengers wait at every stop
Shivering shrouds of fear
Greed pushes first, rape a second
Murder follows third.

Standing room only a demon declares
Room for more upstairs.
Smell foul air on every breath
Ride from here with no returns.

The way to hell is down the road
Traffic lights show green.
Shrills and groans from those below
Crying from all within.

Final checks and all is done
The devil laughs with glee.
Plenty of room for all of you
Entertainment will come free!

Francis Brian Rylance

THE WINDING STREET

There is a winding street with a hill
Where a soap box derby once a year is run
The drivers young and old try and test their skill
The townsfolk urge them on and join in the fun

But on any other day I wonder at this street
And think of all the people this way did tread
And the echo of many passing feet
Of cavaliers and pikesmen and roundhead

Its length I'd say but half a mile
For many years this stage has stood
Flanked by house and cottage brick and tile
Inhabited by townsfolk both bad and good

Small shops where traders sold their wares
Musicians played and danced to entertain
Amused crowds would watch the dancing bears
Over the years the kings and queens did reign

Herdsmen drive cattle of cloven hoof
Milk maids with yoke and pail sell milk
Past lattice window and slated roof
Rich men with buckled shoe and clothes of silk

Atop the hill once stood a picture house tall
In World War II our church was bombed in a raid
A tank scraped along a house wall
The cinema is now a shopping arcade

Maybe a carriage with a lady inside
With a coachman in livery to steer
A beautiful lady along this street did ride
Poor peasants into the windows did peer

The shepherd drives his flock of lambs
Urchins eye apples over a garden wall
Nannies wheel their charges in shiny prams
Smoke drifts from chimneys tall

I wonder of these sort of things
The going on of things gone by
The song thrush on the branch just sings
She does not wonder or even try

Keith Coleman

LINES WRITTEN ON THE AFTERNOON OF SHAKESPEARE'S NATIVITY

It has been a pleasure to read your voice
From since when I heard the words 'What ho!'
I knew some phrases
Like 'to be or not to be,'
Friends, Romans, countrymen,
A horse, a horse, my kingdom for a horse,
Before I read a word of you.

Now you are part of me
Your words and characters
Sit in my soul, they guide my history,
They dictate my words,
Bottom and Shylock, Othello and Macbeth
Were you in them? How much of you was Falstaff?
The mad prince? The bad king?
The lost lovers? Were you in them?

Lost in the words, even in the sonnets
You speak with voices other than your own
We do not know you. Never will.
Did you ever know yourself,
Who spoke with so many voices,
Who inhabited so many fractured, failing persons?

You never wrote a hero without blame
Or villain without reason.

Dead on your birthday,
You never perished
In words
But never appeared
In person when your age was spent
And that is right and proper,
The unity that was you
Burst into plays and poems,
Scenes and characters
That all exist,
Although you cease to be.

Fred Brown

JOHN - THEN GONE (HARD TO IMAGINE)

'All we are saying
(with unkempt locks swaying)
Is give peace a chance'
To Yoko a glance

If peace was his mission
Pen songs his ambition
Let's teen years recall
Scribed lyrics with Paul

Came Ringo and George
'A band we must forge . . .
Great sounds we'll belt out . . .
They'll all twist and shout'

Mankind stopped and stared
At the fab four, mop haired
Cliff and Elvis were warned
Beatlemania's dawned

Their Oyster? The world
As red carpets unfurled
The states proved a cinch
Cracked with barely a flinch

Those nasal twanged tones
Met with girls screams and moans
Whichever the song
Waves of zest gripped the throng

'Twas no great surprise
When these four gifted guys
Having grown somewhat tired
Felt it time they expired

Although now disbanded
On two feet each landed
Their class, as before
Bringing plaudits galore

John's base in New York
A sad loner would stalk
With breath firmly baited
He patiently waited

Disaster then came
Spurred by cravings for fame
Alas, end of gang
As Mark Chapman fired . . . *Bang!*

John Morris

MINDFULNESS

Not long now.
Not too long to wait,
soon the planet will change,
but sadly not our fate, encased
in sorrow, consumed by greed we
undermined our future. In our need
to belong to those who feed, in fear
of being eaten, liberated by the
beating, few can truly say,
they helped the planet
in anyway.

Time now
to forget the
past, learn to help
those who try
so we all
can last.

Jorj Campbell

TITANIC - SHIP OF DREAMS LOST IN

Titanic Titanic, off to New York off we go
The greatest ship afloat fast, not slow
From Queenstown to New York here we come
If only they could see the future, so terrible for some

The ship of dreams, was that really true
If you got a passage, it was a dream for you
If you were third class, you were deep below
Your future was all but written, too late to go

The ship that God himself could not sink
Brave brave words, pity they did not think
I have news for you, iron does not float
Words so so arrogant, why to God did they gloat

Yes the joy of sailing, in the greatest ship ever
On the ocean so cold, makes your heart shiver
Shiver as you may for the Atlantic is deep, so deep
Down into the ocean, for your maker to meet

On and on we sail, three thousands miles to go
The order is full speed, full speed not long to the glancing blow
The fate of Titanic it is sealed, the Angel of Death will come
Many many a life, will never see the morning sun

It is near midnight April 14th, it was so calm that night
The lookouts they did not spot the iceberg, an awesome sight
Late too late Titanic's fate is sealed, never to sail again
Down into the ocean she will go, her passengers she will send

Even God himself could not sink her, so they said
Remember these words, for many souls will soon be dead
There was not enough lifeboats, to save them from the sea
Women and children to the boats, try to save yourself that was the key

What can can you do, when there is no boat for you
Tears cries to God, death will be your fate, sadly true
The band struck up Nearer My God Than Thee, the final song
For into the sea 1500 souls will, will soon be gone

Alas all the lifeboats, they are all gone
It is two in the morning, never will those poor souls see the dawn
Titanic Titanic, she is sinking, sinking fast our God awaits
Bless my wife and children, my life will soon be over, I await my fate

Nearer My God, drifts over the sea my time is near
I have faith I have faith in God from this world my passing, I do not fear
The water is cold so so cold, it is taking the souls of men
Father forgive me my sins, of my soul do not condemn

The ship it is going down, going down by the head
The cries of the living they are fading fast, many must now be dead
The end is near, Titanic raises her stern to the heavens
Down down she goes, like an arrow into the sea she is driven

Titanic Titanic the ship of dreams, she is unsinkable
Only time will tell, sadly to speak such words was that unthinkable
Iron Iron, it does not float we all know that to be true
Only a fool would believe such a thing, surely not you

Allan Brebner

THE O'DYLES

Cool dude 'Croc' O'Dyle and his wife name Delile,
Run a rambling guest house called 'Wide Open Smile,'
Where she serves up pancakes in sugary piles,
And he taxis tourists in trips round the isles.

Their Leprechaun clients from caves in the wild,
All sun seek the beaches and pay dude O'Dyle,
With seaweed and plankton in true, salty style,
But sometimes they slide into jaws at high tide.

And pancakes are left on the shore, high and dry,
Then the youngest O'Dyle, a bright little child,
Turns their clogs into logs which he burns as he scoffs,
Their eats to complete the cool scheme with a smile.

Rosemary Keith

THE SOLDIER BOY

Don't weep dear Mum while I'm away
Don't cry, I've not gone far
Keep in your dreams your thoughts of me
For you're my guiding star
Don't lay your hand across your brow
Don't worry in your heart
We all must answer to the vow
We all must play a part
But carry on in your own way
And if your tears flow
Let the rivers of your heart
Run fast, and feel the glow
Let the ever-changing streams
Wash all your hate away
And let the stars and moonlight gleam
In your eyes each day
I know we're in a foreign land
I known we're here to fight
I know that man is man alone
I know that God is might
And yet I know we'll see it through
And this I know sure
I am coming back to you
Weep not for me, no more
I keep you in my heart each day
And though it's hard, I find
The thoughts and fears of yesterday
The friends I left behind
All are with me here, I know
And in my thoughts, they please
And comfort me and set aglow
A warmth of light release
So sorrow not for me, dear Mum
I'm only one you know
Of the many who have gone before
To keep the flame aglow
I'm not that little boy who left
I'm a man now, you will see

And I know for sure, we will meet again
In freedom, you and me
So weep not for me, Mother dear
As we clasp our hands in peace
For we shall be together once more
When wars of men do cease.

Joan Harris

THE BALLAD OF WOODY GUTHRIE

I am a dead beat,
I've been on Wall Street
For money my fingers were itchin'
I can't stand your bitching,
I couldn't stand the heat so I got out of the devils kitchen,
Got out of the dust bowl,
Before I lost my soul,
Came to New York City,
A town with little pity,
Lost myself in a speakeasy,
Where life is cheap and sleazy,
And the whores are easy,
Picked up my guitar,
In the hope my tomorrows would be breezy,
Sang songs of hope,
For men who couldn't cope,
Said I would go far,
Soon I was the toast of the East Coast,
Sang songs that mattered most,
To the father, son and holy ghost,
In the hope I'd see the setting of the sun,
In this land of fire and gun,
Now my battles won,
As soon as the days begun,
Now Dylan, Seegar, and Baez carry my torch,
To every American's front porch,
Now I go back to where I came from and hence,
The future for Dimaggio and GI Joe,
Is tense.

Alan Pow

HOPE ETERNAL

They say you can hear them
In the breath before dawn
Millions of souls lost in the destruction
Took up by Sunanna in the war to end wars

She heard their dreadful cries
Tormented, twisted and grave
She felt their tortured suffering
No one survived not even the brave

To hold these delicate souls
The box was made of pure gold
Covered in jewels of all colours
Its sight was something to behold

Sunanna hid this box of wonders
Deep within her ample core
She laid down to a deep sleep
A thousand years then a thousand more

They say at the end of the last war
The sun shed blood-red tears
The world went purple black
No one could see in all those years

Well they said they'd learned
No more mistakes start a new
But they never did listen
It seems they never do

You can talk about the horror
Gallons of blood and the gore
But the powers that be don't care
About the awful depravity that's war

Many innocent souls weep
No choice on their side
To see neighbour fight friend
When great powers collide

It's been five thousand long years
Since Sunanna's great sleep
There are not many who remember
The scars of war ran too deep

They say if the souls are released
Great joy and happiness there shall be
And the darkness we now live in
Will be swept away for eternity

This is the related history
My grandmother passed to me
And in my mind's eye something stirred
A thought to find the souls and set free

We live in tunnels dug deep in the earth
My father and brothers keep us close
Many others are not so lucky
Ours is safer by far than most

There are signs you can follow
If you know where to look
Tales of a secret place she found
To hide great steps Sunanna took

With the help of my brother
And his wired box of tricks
We listened at the coming dawn
And picked up the signal, got a fix

You must follow this signal grandma said
But be careful where you go
Do not venture into the open
At all costs you must keep below

I sadly lost my brother
To some bloated ugly thing
It smelt of rotten meat
Festering and squirming within

As it was so fast and so dark
All I could do was run away
I found an old rusty ladder
Upwards and beyond I strayed

I could hear someone screaming
Then realised it was I
And in the grey murky open
All I could do was cry

When I finally stopped sobbing
Up here in this open world
It was not as dark as our tunnels
But still hard to behold

There was grass of a sort
And even flowers and trees
Though it was hard to make out
And I knew I must flee

I could hear running water

And I stumbled on a stream
What else could I do but drink
It turned out better than it seemed

Some sort of fruit was hanging
On a branch dipping down
So hungry I didn't care
What my fate was now

'Stop stupid girl, stop
That tree is diseased
Where did you come from
To now know these things.'

He looked very stooped and old
So I told him my song
I come from underground
From the tunnels of Mong

When he finished listening
He shook his head and laughed
You'd better come home with me
Wild things this way pass

So you look for Sunanna
Oh so long it has been
I thought no one now cared
Fate is a curious thing

I still had my brother's box
But what was very strange
The signal had stopped
As I had entered his domain

I have waited for you long years
Oh dear sister of Mong
Now at last I can have rest
With the end of my song

In the dawn of realisation
He was her and she was him
And I made the eternal trinity
Of this was a certain thing

She carried the light
With the dark I had come
We joined good and bad
Together to become one

Then from its open mouth
Shot a fierce glorious light

It spun and danced around
Joyous singing, a great sight

It went forth straight up
And pierced the gloom to the sky
Spinning round in a circle
This is where the souls choose to die

Such brightness all around
It was wondrous to see
And the world shone in radiance
Blinded for a while but free

They say you can hear them
In the breath before dawn
Still laughing and dancing round
In this new sun that was born.

Marina Wheeler

SONIA'S SONG

Deep, deep, is the hurt of the soul,
Sleep lulls and distraction dulls it.
But it waits
For the floodgates to open
As unbid thoughts wake.
In the grey barren tomb of rejection,
Lies the dream, stillborn from the womb.
Dejections. Hear the tread,
Of the ghost habit step – gone by.
Glimpse the face etched deep
For the memories eye.
Hear the voice – and rejoice not.
No hope! Rise and grope for the thread.
Yes, take up your routine's thread again.
Lock up the pain, the gift was unused, unwanted, unseen.
Trim the lamps, close the door,
All will be as before.
The winter is cold and long,
And no one will hear your song!

Heather Reeves

SAD AND STRANGE

How sad and strange the fate should cruelly arrange
That in the Holy land bloodshed should
Stride the stage as Arab and Jew
Bloody war feel forced to wage . . .
Innocents caught up in this bout of rage
So that where Jesus preached brotherly love
Aggression was set above the state of peace
From which there has been no release
At each the other does incense
Driven out is commonsense

Making an onlooker wish he could
Make them did engage
Wish to switch off the Devil's evil cooker
Or better still, on the combatants impose his will
That peace he might swiftly instil
Then no longer would Arab nor Jew hotly kill
The fighters for two millennia is exercising war mania
Might then sight paradise and finally cease to fight
With all their might believing that only they were right
To witness them shaking the other's hand
Would be supremely and sublimely grand
Allowing the world to witness a calm
And peace-loving land.

Onlookers wish
Making the onlooker wish
He wasn't sitting on the fence
Making ordinary man wonder who did the Devil page
Clearly, searingly he has shown his hand
Continued to create bloody nonsense
Deranged by Dabolo it is plain
Planned to cause maximum pain
In order therefore is the prayer
Wishing Christ would return there to
That now unholy land where plainly the
Devil has shown his hand
A real devilish stew
No one has a clue how chaos grew
Arab and Jew consequently the other slew
Over the Holy Land blood freely spew
Sins of the fathers like decay gathers
How sad and strange the fate should cruelly
Arrange that in the Holy land bloodshed should
Stride the stage as Arab and Jew

Bloody war feel forced to wage . . .
Innocent caught up in this bout of rage
So that where Jesus preached brotherly love
Aggression was set above the state of peace
From which there has bene no release
As each the other does incense
Driven out is commonsense
Making an onlooker wish he could
Wish to switch off the Devil's evil cooker
Or better still, on the combatants impose his will
That peace he might swiftly instill
Then no longer would rab nor Jew hotly kill
The fighters for two millennia is exercising war mania
Might then sight paradise and finally cease to fight
Will all their might believing that only they were right
To witness them shaking and sublimely grand
Allowing the world to witness a calm
And peace-loving land.

Graham Watkins

BEN SHAW

I searched every shop in Crouch Hill
I couldn't find Ben Shaw
Till eventually I found him in a nest
On display a mile away
In Hornsey Lane
Yes I bagged Dandelion
Cloudy and soda
They weren't going to be left
I weighed heavy
Ben Shaw pulling me down
When I left him out of the bag
Pop he sprayed me in the eyes I had him
The Jubilee was nearing
Derby runners getting ready
I might take Ben Shaw to the Epsom Races and crown him
When I win with diamonds and Burdock.

John Scanlan

SIGNS OF INTELLIGENCE THE FIRST MAN TO FALL TO EARTH

The Egyptian goddesses rise and sigh
Sighting a beautiful golden egg
Falling from the heavenly clear sky
Landing gracefully in the Red Seas
Breaking the calm surface of the salt blue hue
Drifting to the shore upon a light breeze.

From the 'egg' emerges the great awaited one
The Egyptians salute and worship the sun
Sun God of the kingdoms of 'Ancient Egypt'
And almighty Zeus to classical Greece
He says the one who has come in peace
And has traversed the heavens is Ra;
The Egyptian court and Ra become engaged in talk
Ra is welcome royalty, the sacred hawk
Protected by the symbols of the sun
And the powers of the lotus flower and the reed
The Egyptians now have all the knowledge they need.

That is how the circle of progress began
The first to fall to, pearl, Earth was a man.

Graham Peter Metson

SENSES

Have you ever thought?
What a beautiful gift your senses are?
The eyes, in which you take a snap shot of
A moment that stays with you, forever in life.
The ears, through which you hear,
Spoken words of love or admiration.
The laughing of your friends,
And the feelings of people spread through sound.
The smell, of fresh flowers,
Growing in the ground.
Tasting, a texture within your pallet,
Filling the emptiness of your stomach,
Melting your hunger away.
Touch, feeling the softness.
Of warm sand beneath your feet,
The type that's hot to walk on in the heat.
All these are an essential part of life,
Whether evolved genetically,
Or an act of Christ.

Emma-Louise Gardner

AFTER ARMAGEDDON

Mole beside your burrow,
Blinking at the day,
Now the world had ended,
What's there left to say?

Yes, you have survived them,
Skulking under sod,
Monstrous clouds like mushrooms,
Making mock of God.

What's this ghastly greyness?
Where's the greenness fled?
Why is all around you,
Scorched and seared and dead?

Luckier he who lingered
Staring at the sky,
Sighing, 'Suns can perish,
So, why shouldn't I?'

Eileen-Margaret Kidd

A DARK TWIST

Have you ever held
The cold dark night
Held it so tight its brittle bones
Break in your arms?

The mind moves its own
Jumbled thoughts around
Until its emptiness is left in the middle
A game of solitaire

Days of the past go
Through your mind
A reel of film
On repeat constantly

Limits of sadness
Do not exist within depression
It overflows from the conscious mind
As tears

Your life is like a wilting flower
Blown apart by cruel winds
Consumed or thinking of history

Time to hold the familiar dark night
Away from the prying sun
Alone, invisible
Like me goodnight.

John Ball

EVE THE PLANT OF LIFE

The Garden of Eden rose from its sleep of tranquil peace,
Night had slipped back to the heavens to give way to the innocent dawn
Which is older than yesterday, younger than tomorrow.

Birds were singing to their little ones,
Butterflies opened wings of softness silk.
Peacocks roamed freely looking for true love,
To complete their existence of life.

Christ's soul was in the lily's heart waiting to be conceived,
Essence of roses captured the air.
Eve sat with long hair shining against the water of eternity,
Cleanse my soul knowing it will make me pure again,
Let me taste the water of your sweetness.
My mind will be above this pain of endless time.

Forgive the things my eyes make me see – I will rise above once more,
Feeling cool essence of water like a thousand white roses,
That have been kissed with laughing rain,
Your colour of no importance,
Let the purity of the water turn to wine,
You are part of me, without you I would surely die.

Precious water – may you exist forever,
Like diamonds on untouched snow
Only you have the gift to give everlasting peace and life.

Looking at the serpent curled neatly around the tree of destiny.

'Taste the fruit of red lust. Be dazzled by the jewels of rubies,
That beckon to your call,' he said.

She thought, 'I need to have free-will, my own identity.'
The apple mingled with her blood like wine.
The serpent shed his skin, God cried.
The sky rained tears of dismay.

Barbara Posner

A COLE QUALITY

It was while reading Sammy's Buo tribute
This title said hi there
For within each of Glady's and Lionel children
This quality can be found
This selfless quality
This quality so often astound
For Sammy wrote
'Syl would give his last shirt off his back'
this was Syl alright!
Family members and friends who wrote tributes for Ionie
Wrote of her selflessness
Her generosity and her warmth
This is a Cole quality
This wasn't acquired
But was inherited from birth.

For our dear mama and pappa
Has this selfless quality
Forever thinking of others
And leaving themselves short
Maybe they too
Had it passed down
From generation gone by.

I remember my first U.S $5.00
Clifford had given it to me when I was 14
I gave my friend Amethyst one whole dollar
The first she had ever held
And boy was her smile bright.

I have this vision of my mama
Going to her mahogany glass cabinet
And taking out all of her best china
Chefeta and Zelma trying to stop her
'Mama, Mama, you can't take all of her best things'
But Mama wasn't having any of that
It was nothing but the best for her
Mama took her gifts to church
To put them under the Christmas tree
Mama left full of the joys of Christmas
But she came back filled with misery
She was angry and spitting fire fumes
For the gifts she received
Was a box of matches and a hairnet
Mama cursed and cursed

'Is so little they think of me'
That day in my 8 years old frame
I felt empathy for my mother.

As the years went by
I came to realise
That a box of matches can save your life
But a china plate can't
So the hurt I felt for my mother
Is now subdued.

A Cole quality
Our selflessness
A Cole trademark for sure
Has left other astounded
And saying wow!

Karty Cole

WITHDRAWALS

My keepers search here and seek there
They've been all round the zoo, everywhere,
I'm sat here on a form,
And I'll do you no harm,
Cos I only came out for a fag,
I'll feel better when I've had a drag
It's a no smoking zoo,
So what else can I do?
This craving is driving me mad.
When I was a young ape aged three
You tested these ciggies on me,
Now I've got an affliction,
It's called an addiction,
I need nicotine, don't you see,
Because everyone's run off in fright,
There's no one to give me a light,
And it's beyond a joke,
When you're craving a smoke,
Now I'm rapidly getting uptight.
So I think it's the best thing to do,
To toddle straight back to the zoo,
They might give me a match,
But more likely a patch,
So I'll kick up a fuss, wouldn't you?

Marian Tonge

YOU THOUGHT

Am I to get a night there of,
That I can call my own,
It seems so like, it's not somehow,
Where the might is sown.
Maybe not, or maybe yes,
It's all a guess, or maybe swot,
For if I don't think what, when of,
I sure as seem forgot,
What was it now, can't really say,
Because my mind is blank,
Do mean that, just thought of nothing,
And haven't you to thank,
But then again I hadn't thought,
Or maybe it was taught,
But not to me, the lesson's show,
Now just can't you see,
You what, you don't, can't think of it,
Or nothing to say,
I've said enough, ah that's just tough,
I will not say, no more.
If it's a continuance of what,
I hadn't said before that,
Then what where I come nor go,
It must be, new moon there,
Or could it be, or should its plea,
Ever I should care,
I'm really mixed twice, and gathered once,
Or was it, three or four,
I haven't a clue, it's all down to you,
Should not have said it before,
Before what, how would I know,
I'm only writing, because I can't sleep,
If you're as good, as you say you were,
You wouldn't let me go on,
Possibly not, an hour it will dawn.

Hugh Campbell

MY PARALLEL WORLD

I lay me down to sleep
The wonders of the day to keep,
But I know that for the whole night long,
To my parallel world I do belong.

For dreams we are told are thoughts you unfold,
Just events in brains computer bold,
But me oh dear me no those nights I can explain,
When I go out and about, I'm on another plain.

I speak and I am spoken to
Colours I see so clear and of every hue,
Even those senses of feel and touch,
For I am alive out there, I know that much.

A time when my arm through a wall would not go
A man appeared and said, 'You can, concentrate' I did and lo,
All of me into a room through the wall,
He stands with me in a large hall.

I see a mahogany staircase to another floor,
A woman in white standing there by a door.
She beckoned, I follow, floating up to the woman in white,
I feel her presence in my body taking me into the night.

Across a river to the quayside quarter,
We walked there only ankle-deep in water,
A man sitting beneath a tree,
Come my son sit with me.

'I will take you to a time and place'
his hand in mine through time we go apace,
to a time on rocks in Saturn's rings,
there hieroglyphics he touched those things.

There are some who when told just smile and pout,
But I know of a life that is real when I am out and about,
For in that parallel world where I am me
Life is so real that when I awake exhausted I will be.

John Clarke

THE FLEETING WONDER CALLED . . .

Childhood; that long ago memory of a full moon
In a black velvet star-filled sky; that all to soon
Would dwindle to the stark light of day
We never thought that would go away
Forever, with the flowing years . . .
That time of laughter and tears
Seaside fun and games galore
Like tiddlywinks, marbles, 'bang on door
And run away; postman's knock, blind man's buff
Lots of crazy, but just kids stuff . . .
Learning to ride a bike, making daisy chains
Sleeping in a garden tent, getting wet when it rains
Building a snowman, making castles with sand
Watching a birthday magician, amazed at his sleight of hand.
School days in the playground, races on sports day
Dancing round a may pole in the merry month of May.
Dandelion clocks, picking violets and primroses in the spring
Bluebell woods and picnics, flying high on a swing.
We took it all for granted, thought it would last forever
Did not know the passing of time, comes to us to sever
The tie of the fleeting wonder called childhood
Those halcyon days when life was so good . . .
That long ago memory of a moon on the wane
And places we have been, and cannot go again.

Valerie Hall

WE ALL KNOW THE ANSWERS

We all know all the answers
It's the questions we can't find.

My thoughts aren't dark
Just flowing free
Abundantly insistently.

We all know all the answers
It's the questions we can't find.

They tap against my head
They tap against my waking head
They tap against my sleeping head
They tap.

We all know all the answers
It's the questions we can't find.

Worse than dreams of smothered pigs
Are ones of slashing wrists,
Watching the blood run red
With sacrificial arms out stretched
They touch my waking dreams
And seep into my waking head.

We all know all the answers
It's the questions we can't find.
But you are blind to my pain
And cannot see the hurt in me.
I will not let you see.

Suicide is not the answer
It's just another question.
We all knew all the answers
It's the questions we can't find.

Clare Todd

MY HOUSE IS FULL OF LEGS AND FEET

My house is full of legs and feet, male of which are four.
While one he walks on his own two feet, the others walk on paws.
The one my son my little man, growing straight and tall.
For him I'll do my very best because that's what mums do after all.

The others they are dogs you see, not man's best friend but mine.
And even though they rule the roost, I love them all the same.
They love me back of this I'm sure for they are my very best friends,
Although the feeding, cleaning, walking never seems to end.

Now I've told of just a few for if you look amongst the boys, the girls come into view.
Not more I hear you laugh, but the girls they equal out the boys and form the other half.
Not just on four legs but on two my daughter I must mention,
For though the dog outweigh the kids she still gets my attention.

While my son grows strong and tall my daughter, small, petite.
Like the dogs their opposite right down to the size of feet.
These legs are not the only ones to walk these crowded floors,
For in to this comes another two feet.

A daughter with a grandson on all fours again the numbers equal out.
No more I hear you say, but into this there's just one more it's me at last OK.

You may think me mad in all of this utter chaos, there's not calm or bliss,
But in the setting of the sun.

I thank God for them all.
I love them, everyone.

Deanna James

SMOKE TREE

The Smoke Tree strong and vulnerable,
Reigned Monarch of the shrubs and trees,
His smoky plumes mere lazy puffs,
Swaying and waving in the breeze,
He reminisced all summer long,
Recounting all he'd heard and seen,
When homes were built on meadowland,
And lawns were laid with turf so green,
Quite settled in his patch of ground,
He now felt loved and pampered,
His silhouette was trim and neat,
Gone were the fronds that hampered,
He looked with favour at the trees,
The myriad shrubs of evergreen,
Inhaled the heady fragrances,
Amongst the flowers he did preen,
His garden was so beautiful,
To every budding plant he spoke,
His ancient language Treelian,
So musical did not provoke,
The plants to pull up roots and die,
But rather helped the parched and worn,
Who listened and tried to revive,
No longer looking lost forlorn,
Many songbirds stopped to rest,
And eat their snacks within the tree,
Sometimes they'd play at hide-n-seek,
With their offspring quite carefree,
In time all plants spoke Treelian,
Their stories drifted in the breeze,
By day and night their whispering,
Sighed mellow music through the trees.

Lorna Troop

THE SILENT PROTECTOR

Penicillin has saved many lives
By killing harmful bacteria
But long before the discovery of penicillin
Other silent killers were at work more superior

Saving lives by destroying bacteria
These silent killers are white blood cells
These hard workers are God's way
Of protecting us from disease to keep us well

We don't know how many invasions they have stopped
Or how many lives they have saved
They receive little or no recognition for all their good
One should stand in awe and be truly amazed

The Lord gets similar treatment
Being blamed when things go awry
He seldom gets credit for all the things
That go right as our lives pass by

Daily events such as getting up and going out
Going to work, and mixing with strangers
Returning home safely, no one knows how many times
God has protected us that day from dangers

When we consider all the wonderful things
That God does on our behalf each day
Our list of praises should be much longer
Than our list of petitions we say.

Catherine M Armstrong

IDLE THOUGHTS

Oh idle thoughts that race around my head
Synthesising dreams of fears in an imaginary world
I wonder if they could realise happiness instead

Of a constant cycle of impoverished life
Would it be that on the horizon a ray of hope
That the moonlight's ember, shine effervescent
To a hue of feelings with which we could cope
And not scramble around with idle thought

Would it be that reality and dreams intertwine
Oh how surreal a vision of beauty and light
That the love surrounding you is forever mine
Through eternity and the circle complete
And not touch on idle thought

Could we not dream of a utopian life
Where there is no colour, creed to slander
And barely no gnarled hearts worn by strife
But a world of vision through a telescope eye
All seeing in idle thought

That mistakes were soon mended and clear
No room for error just perfection and love
Come thoughts, come hither bring yourself near
To transcend all aspects of a transitional world
And dream in idle thought

Where society and mankind's minds clasp
That life is worthwhile, for living not war
And translucent thoughts within our grasp
Live as one, unite in peace, love to this world
And finite in idle thought.

Annie Stubbs

BETRAYAL OF TRUST

The love is still there, I know it,
Rooted deep in my soul, it will always endure.
But for now, the trust has gone
Disappeared without trace.
Like mist in the warmth of the morning sun.
The sharp angry voice, the harsh words in print,
The long agonising months of silence,
Have shocked me to the core of my being,
The delicate flowers of trust have withered
In the face of the raging blasts
Of cold anger.

For so long over the years our friendship,
Had been strong and untouchable –
Talking, sharing, knowing that
We could find support and love in each other,
Bad times, good times, the bond was strong,
Always to be relied upon, how could it
Ever be otherwise, we thought.
But neglect, family tensions and friction,
Gradually pervaded our relationship like a creeping paralysis,
Until the final spark ignited the explosion of anger.

Now I feel lost and bewildered as if in an alien land,
With an aching black hole inside, so unsure of the territory we are now in.
Wary and frightened of making the wrong move,
Not knowing which direction to take.
Only knowing that the love remains intact,
But the trust has been betrayed.
Where do we go from here?
There is a seed of hope in my heart,
Hope that we will come through,
That we will weather the storm,
Because of the love which endures.

But trust is like a wounded animal,
Once it has been hurt – it will take,
Months or even years to coax it back again,
It needs to be nurtured slowly with
Patience, forbearance, caring words and actions,
So too, there needs to be a mutual desire,
To restore and re-make the relationship,
Then trust may grow again and having been,
Forged in the fire of experience and forgiveness,
A stronger and deeper bond may emerge and

We can move forward again, but
I am growing old and time is short.

June Smith

THE GROCIAN

The petrol died up and we were all stranded
Until that day when the 'Grocian' landed
It stared at our car with the smoke coming out
And asked, 'Is this how you all get about?'
We gaped at the thing with enormous behind
Whatever we said, we had better be kind
An alien like this might well be quite cruel
And we'd only stopped here just to search for some fuel
He suddenly smiled, said he knew of our plight
With kind outstretched arms, he held us all tight
'We Grocians used to drive round in cars
And drink and smoke and frequent bars
We lived in houses, went to school
Enjoyed ourselves mostly as a rule
Then we discovered a better idea
We'd keep our powers in our rear
I can't remember when it started
But one day King Grocian loudly farted
He was gone like the wind, at the speed of sound
But he landed quite safely, just bounced on the ground
So we perfected technique and just at will
We can fart a little to get over a hill
For journeys of distance, we do need to start
To get to the coast needs a jolly big fart
So we carry some spares so just to be ready
The smell's too bad because it's unleady
If we run out of fuel, and we're in a hurry
There's the Queen Raj of Grocian does a takeaway curry
So take my advice, from now on use your bum
'Cause after a while it's soon becomes numb'
And then he was gone, what a way to depart
Over the hill with a half-hearted fart.

Graham Hayden

IN PRAISE OF TODAY

With all the doom and gloom and dire despair,
I'll sing a song of praise and comfort,
The switch of the switch, the turn of the screw,
The opening of the mighty can,
For this is today!
Our convenience have given us freedom
To think; perhaps too much, but reflect;
For us, we miss the shadows of the flickering fire,
We also miss the icy draughts of ice-cold,
Which invaded passages from room to room,
We miss the long excursions to the privy,
With candlelight held high in fear of bats at night,
We now sleep at night in warmth,
No more the icy morning,
With our breath before us yawning,
In white mists, so it snowed last night,
We miss the frost flowers on windowpanes,
We also miss chilblains, and the feverish dressing,
In bed; before we put the reluctant foot,
Into the cold morning of bleak mid-winter.

Aside from this and for myself,
For thrice has death called me on his rolecall,
And thrice has been eluded by the modern drug,
So I met him eye to eye and laughed,
In past days the grave would have claimed myself,
And I would never have known the joys that come with travel,
In youth one read the National Geographical
In quiet, musty library, in mittens,
Dreaming of other lands and people
But today, we realise our childhood dreams,
And see and feel and experience at firsthand
The mountains tops; and walk on snow above the valleys,
The air thin, but pure and unpolluted,
How marvellous, what grandeur there,
Even better than books, the true reality,
We board the plane, itself a wonder,
And travel fast, static it seems,
And view clouds below, in fantastic formation,
While we are bathed in the eternal sun,
Dropping down the islands show,
Like blotting paper in a silver sea,
Otherwise we go, and visit ancient Rome.
Better than dreams, again, the reality of this,

The mightiness of empires gone,
And put a foot where the almighty past was once,
In cool colonnades, in ruins now,
So treading on the past, history seems a moment gone,
For how could our forebears know these joys?
It was then the lot of common man,
To work and toil, begat and die –
For most not even the compensation of the written word,
So we, the inheritors of past peasants' lot,
Should take our pleasure now, or not forget,
The hardships past and poverty stark.
We are informed by radio and by TV,
Of other peoples, other lands,
Perhaps we see other nations rising;
To claim creature comforts and freedom of thought and word,
And why not? Providing these inanimate things
Become the tools; and not the Gods of men -
Therein the danger lies; we are poised on the brink -
'A little learning is a dangerous thing'
That's true - for we should have the sense,
To use science for our own ends and rejoice
In the freedom of our choice,
And choose wisely; and not tempt
Our own annihilation.

Betty Shipway

THE CLOWN

Mirrored,
Cragfull face
Of hagfull mouth,
Yawning,
Tired eyes,
Cried outside emptiness,
Still, void suckling,
Of wisdom,
Unstill head,
Of unwed memories,
Painted clown,
Of downtrodden
Askew ideas, fears
Of unfulfilled
Completive years.

Task of your mask
To dance with you
Unfurtile, futile dances
In secondary person,
To improve of worsen
With the unstable illusion
Of your own reflection
Time's imperfection.

Sally Plumb

SIGHT

Sitting looking thro' the mist,
Trying to see more clearly.
That now is my life.
To see again, I wish for dearly.
Once I could see the lovely flowers,
That grow here in the garden,
Now at least, I have the scent,
When guided by the warden.
It means so much in life
To see the things around us.
To see, to read, is what I used to do,
But now I have to touch.
Memories are a blessing,
In my mind I can look back,
There I can see in my head,
The joys and the sorrows,
Which long ago I shared.
Our sight we take for granted,
I know that once I did,
Until it's lost, we do not realise,
The awful lonely cost.
Pity is something quite unwanted,
To be treated just the same,
Is what I hope for, and is my aim.

Grace Maycock

THE CHARGE OF THE CAR BRIGADE

Half an inch, half an inch,
Half an inch onward,
All into the traffic jam
Rode the six hundred.
Forward the car brigade!
Oh not again they prayed:
All into the traffic jam
Drove the six hundred.

Forward the car brigade!
Was there a driver dismayed?
Even though passengers knew
Someone had blundered:
Theirs not to rant and cry,
Theirs not to reason why,
Theirs but to sit and sigh:
Into the traffic jam
Drove the six hundred.

Cars to the right of them,
Cars to the left of them
Cars in front them
Stuttered and shunted:
No use the traffic news,
Only serves to confuse,
Into the jaws of chaos,
Into the hell of queues,
Drove the six hundred.

Flashed at by car and van,
Flashed at by every man,
Our day out down the pan,
Will we every get there
We all wondered:
Baking in our stuffy car
We haven't got very far
In these hours.
Heat from the road tar
Smells as engines thundered.
Should we turn back thought
The six hundred.

Cars to the right of them,
Cars to the left of them,
Cars behind them,
Stuttered and shunted:

Turn off the traffic news,
I'm going to blow a fuse,
Traffic signs that confuse
In this grid-locked chaos
In this hell of queues,
None was moving,
In this six hundred.

When will the traffic fade?
Where's the improvement made.
All the world wondered.
'Honour the promises made!
Honour the taxes paid,'
Said the six hundred.

Sue Gerrard

THE HOUSE OF LORDS

The crow's feet in frost
Caw-caw in the trees
Walking in the swanky style
Jet-black soot pitch-black
Crows, jackdaws swaying
Calling over in twigs leaves
The weekend is scraggy
Long endless still goes out
In zone of time of roller cast
To give permission to calmness
Becoming mature in haze pockets
What help do they give brusque?
Prime ministers have come in
When the queen has reigned
A stamp cost sixpence
New money palmed hands
Algerelma died out with the half
A crown, there is no help
Around unless someone can
Raise the dead.
The crows warned danger.

John Sheehy

ODE TO A LITTLE GIRL

A little girl lost
At such a cost
One evening in May
Maddie's away
Five years ago
Where did she go?
Nobody knows
The mystery grows
Brother and sister
O how they miss her
Was it God's plan
To vindicate Man
And what of a woman
Who only is human
Remember her child
So tender and mild
Still in her youth
Where is the truth?
Is she in Rome?
Madeleine come home
Where else can she be
Is she in me?
Can I give her back
When children I lack
A little girl found
Her name's all around
Safe in my heart
Never to part . . .

Norma Anne MacArthur

AFFLUENZA 2012

As Affluenza sweeps the nation,
How can we achieve salvation?
Rags and riches just don't mix,
Addicts of the materialisation fix.

When did hopes in their array,
Shift to jealousy and dismay?
How did dreams drift and turn,
To footballers' lives; money to burn?

As stocks and shares deteriorate,
The fountain of riches becomes desolate,
Not the pounds, shillings and pence,
But the investments we make into our own sense.

The fuel our ancestors struggled to save,
Wasted and squandered. The situation is grave.
The fuel of love and life and health,
Chemically changed by seduction of wealth.

The symptoms of this pandemic are clear,
Greed and gadgets, wanting and fear,
They take away our ability,
To enjoy life and just feel free.

So what we must find is the cure,
To end this ongoing consumption war,
To unchain us from the toil and strife,
That has become our daily life.

Open your windows, open your eyes,
Look into the future, enjoy the blue skies,
Don't take for granted all that you are,
Who cares what you drive – it's only a car!

Laura Muskin

LADIES WHO LUNCH DOWN LEAFY LANES

Down leafy lanes
Ladies who lunch
Have heard, somewhere,
Of having brunch . . .

Ladies who lunch
Are not surprised
At this, but find it
Too Americanised:

Not to their taste:
Mealtimes should be
Specifically:
First, morning tea,

A slice of toast;
Lunch: one-fifteen;
Dinner at eight;
Tea in-between.

Those leafy lanes
Ladies traverse
In sturdy cars,
With bulging purse

To seek delights
In country inns:
Steak and ale pie,
One – or two! – gins . . .

Then, sated, they
Stroll over to
Last visit to
The ladies loo . . .

One, Vera, says
'I had a hunch
They would provide
A lovely lunch.'

And, really, Pru
Has to agree:
'That apple tart!
Light as can be!'

Ladies who lunch
Admire the view
When driving back,
Then bid adieu . . .

Together say:
'See you next week,'
Bestow a kiss
On the other's cheek.

Ladies who lunch –
Quite separately
Kick off their shoes
At home, with tea . . .

And dream of next
Weeks escapade,
And leafy lanes,
And pleasant glade,
And home-baked pie,
And G & T . . .
And home again
By half-past three . . .

Dorinda MacDowell

THE RARE ABILITY OF GOD

I hid the word. I challenge to my will, I walk the plain path and never desert the hill if I was an angel. I fear no challenge, I pass through any struggle. And never desert My God.
I walk, I hide the word. And till the time comes to say it.
And in a worthwhile struggle spend my days.
I master even challenge. I feel the pain of sorrow.
I feel the pain of sickness.
And answers to my call.
And in a worthwhile struggle spend my days.
The worlds needs men and women to fight for the truth.
It takes a braver heart.
And a stronger faith.
To fight the battle.
For peace.
Brother. Sister. Mother. Father. Stretch out your hand love your children.
Is there any love left in this world?
I search my soul and my soul says yes but I look with my eyes and I can't see any yet.

Imogen Lindo

THE BRIEF

'For the noble life you led,
I am giving you now rebirth.
For the task that lies ahead
You are going back to Earth.

It is not just for you alone,
But for everyone around.
Show them how it can be done
How goodness can be found.'

'Will I return the same old me
The same old form and face?'
'No, the world will be your family,
You will dwell in every place.

You will need help where ere you go,
You will have to choose some others,
Teach them all the things you know,
And treat all men as brothers.'

'How then can I best prepare,
For the work that I must do?'
'You will see the need when you get there
I know you will see it through.'

'Will me, my friends not recognise
As once they used to do?'
'They will not know you with their eyes
But they will know that it is you.

No mortal frame to it contain,
Your spirit will be far reaching
When you take up your work again
They'll know you by your teaching.

Reach out to those who have not heard,
Tell them the wondrous story,
Go now my son and spread my word
And fill their hearts with glory.'

Robert Hogg

THE HOLY ONES

Absolute the slaves who carry burdens,
For 'nine to fivers are the salt of the Earth'
Kings are clearly there for decoration
As Man has ever needed his façade
Heavy crowns and glittering treasures burden
And chain them to a life of sitting down
But the superb splendour of the naked soul
When married to the wonderful works of nature
Far outreach the puny works of Man
And lavatories being one of his better creations
Are cleaned by the 'Holy Ones' who removed the stains
And bottoms are a beautiful, natural creation
Though different shapes they're more or less the same
The waste that lactates from these splendid bottoms
Soils the pan and then goes down the drain
Without the noble breed of lavatory cleaners
We'd be repulsed by other people's stains
Though thrones are used by kings with jewellery
Slaves and kings all sit on lavatory bugs
But the king runs when the cistern's faulty
Yet servants do more work when the system clogs
Without his slaves his Majesty's royal bottom
Would be in a pretty awful state
So rever the ones who clean the toilets
For without them stench would be our fate
Kings are only puppet slaves of the people
Whilst people spend find lives as the monarch's slaves.

Joan Elizabeth Blissett

LOVE'S TRUE DEVOTION

Love's chattering away,
Around a corner, down a lane,
Now absent from past attentions,
Content to be amused,
Leaving hearts broken in two,
And often all askew.

Entranced by its exploits,
Of piercing hearts with darts,
Dipped in narcotic doping emotion,
Love may stay away for years.

Then when least expected,
Return with pleasure, pain potion,
To inoculate anew
Destroying all resistance,
With the eyes, face, smile, voice,
Of a person that's all to you.

But then love,
Keep best its company and charm,
Extracts its mirth, affection mesmerising presence,
To go away and chatter – quite alone.

Colin Coles

COWES WEEK

I dream of sailing yachts and bows
First over line at Hallowed Cowes
Their beeby crews work out in gyms
Oh the endless summer Pimms!

A sea of blazers greets the eye
Complete with dashing Eton tie
Outfit is so tailor made
Pretty girlfriends on parade.

Such comradeship in set to last
Nail school colours to the mast
Fulham Broadway swamping town
Plus playboys of a foreign crown.

This August idlyll – over – when
Back to London – 'City' men
Remember fondly – favourite bar
Solent sailors on par.

Steve Glason

DEMENTIA

I hold her hand,
Trying to understand.

It must be like being,
Waiting, dreaming,
In some timeless land.

Every now and again,
She'll squeeze my hand.

Try to say something,
But the words emerge,
In a strange language,
Except when we sing.

Sometimes, aware of problems,
Deep within her dreams,
Flashes of past reality,
Return to her, sadly.

And she will hold my hand and cry,
And sadly so will I.

Stan Solomons

THE HOUSEWIFE'S LAMENT

I am always a believer in 'Equal Pay' for all,
But as a 'Low-Achiever,' all my wages are quite small.
So, before I have to cease work, I shall make my feelings plain,
And resort to doing 'Piece Work' – (What I lose, I'm sure to gain).

I gave my husband, Willie, a run-down on what I do,
And although he says I'm silly – he's agreed to pay what's due!
So, drying out his undies when he gets caught in a shower,
Will be listed under 'Sundries' – and will cost two quid an hour,
And to wash his mobile scooter, which is full of mud and grime,
Will be priced on my computer, at a tenner for my time.

My digging skills I'll banish . . . No more pulling up his spuds,
Our 'Sex-Life' will just vanish . . . 'til he comes up with the goods,
And although he'll not be happy, well, I really do not care,
And he'd better make it snappy . . . for there's housework everywhere.

So here's the ultimatum, either he brings out his purse,
Or he's heading for cremation . . . or a fate for him . . .
Much worse!

Dorothy Rawnsley

PLEASANT DREAMS

In dreams you can walk as tall as the sky
Just sit and watch the world go by
Be Lord and master of all you desire
Ride along, on chariots of fire
No violence invades the dreams you weave
Nothing that makes you weep and grieve
You can go from home to Rome in a flash
With bottomless pockets, no need for cash
If all our dreams came miraculously true
What would reporters find to do

The aristocrat on millionaires row
Dreams of possessions and where to go
The businessman in his tie and suit
Dreams of the stock exchange, lots of loot
The harrassed housewife alone in her den
Dreams of a beach, filled with hunky men
While the homeless waif and tramp on the street
Dreams of a fire and something to eat.

Dora Watkins

WOLF

(For Phillip
Tranquil rest and peaceful sleep
your memory alive I'll always keep
love you forever our kid)

Moonlight above, forest below
Shadows by night
Stealthily they go
Running with the pack
Grey, white or black
A wolf in the wild
Like nature's child
Howling at the moon
On the hunt soon
The sound of their call
From high in the hills
Recognized by all
As heartbeat stills
Whether deer or fowl
They fear that howl
Tracking their prey
It won't get away
Like a military drill
Wolves make their kill
Those hypnotic almond eyes
Crimson blood on snow lies.

Darren Morton

UNTITLED

I
Do try
To be positive
And aim to live
Keeping an open, alert mind
Leaving bigotry and bias far behind,
Nourishing hopes, planning for the future
Welcoming the chance for adventure,
Never without a look
Or resolute outlook
To remain
Sane.

Sheila Juliet Dodwell

CARROT AND ORANGE

It was that damned soup. I thought I was over the separation,
The gulf, the loss, and then just when I didn't expect it,
There you were again.
Carrot and orange.

I hadn't tried it until that night in your cottage,
A new starter, a soup I didn't know. I confessed my ignorance,
Then at the first spoonful my taste buds sang with wonder
And the best ingredient, of course, was love.

Now, in a restaurant with a friend
The only love is that of the chef for perfection;
But oh! That taste! The contrast:
The sweet carrot and the tart orange, so good together,

And I saw again the candlelight, the curve of your lips
As you smiled at me, the little wrinkling of your nose
As you met a less than full blended piece of orange . . .
It's over now. Two years ago. I cook a little these days.

More than I did before, but I've not had the courage
To make that soup; so this was like lightning.
A good restaurant, a good friend, but not
One of our evenings, stretching out long before us
No, just once again, briefly, heart aflame, eyes closed in memory;
Carrot and orange. My love, my lost, last love.

Geoffrey Speechly

DAUGHTER

I sit and stare at my silent phone,
I will it to ring or bleep, but Bex is quiet as the grave,
Her promise, she won't keep!

She never lets me in her world,
Though I've tried and tried and tried,
Every time, she cancels, there's another bit of me that's died.

She keeps me hanging on the edge,
But never lets me in, I wish I could be the one
She wants to spend time with,
But I'm just the last resort you see,
She really, really don't want me!

I wish that she would call me, and ask me over,
For a meal, or take me to the movies,
But, she don't care how I feel,
I'm only used, when no one else will come to help her out,
She don't want complications or to know what I'm about!

I wish she'd buy a little gift, and just give it to me with love,
But she's so wrapped up in all her life,
I'll never get it, and that's tough!
She was the sweetest baby
Such a loving little child,
But I lost her, when she grew up,
She's been gone so many years,
To be so close, and yet, so far,
I've cried so many tears!

Oh Bexxy, please come back an be my daughter dear,
Cos, one day my love, you'll look around,
And find that I'm not here!
Why can't you see into my heart,
And see my pain and fear,
Why can't you hear me crying?
Oh Bex,
I'm here, I'm here, I'm here . . .

Rosemary Childs

WHO?

Who was born of a virgin two thousand years ago,
And visited by shepherds, their faces aglow?
Who did the wisemen seek being guided by a star,
And paid homage to when they journeyed from afar?
Who in the temple did Simeon and Anna give praise,
And who had they been waiting for all of their days?
Who did The Holy Spirit rest upon like a dove,
And who was the one, full of grace, mercy and love?
Who fasted for forty days and forty nights,
Being tempted by Satan and shown all his rights?
Who was the one who turned water to wine,
And said, 'My father is the gardener and I am the vine'?
Who made the disciples fishers of men,
And taught them to become like little children?
Who made the lame to leap, jump and walk,
And who made the dumb able to talk?
Who touched the leper with his healing hand,
And who was the one in such high demand?
Who raised the dead up from the grave,
And who was so gentle, kind, meek and brave?
Who fed five thousand with two fish and five loaves,
And who was the one they came to in droves?
Who walked on water and amazed them all,
And who was at everyone's beck and call?
Who calmed the storm and said, 'Peace be still,'
And who was the one doing God's will?.
Who preached the sermon up on the mount,
And who performed miracles, too many to count?
Who said to sinners, 'Come eat with me,'
And who was transfigured and witnessed by three?
Who came to Jerusalem on Palm Sunday,
Riding a donkey and leading the way?
Who chased the money lenders out of God's house,
And never harmed anyone, not even a mouse?
Who at the final last supper broke bread,
And said, 'Take of this wine, my blood which is shed?'
Who said to one there, 'Leave your glory is now,
You must go right now to fulfil your vow?'
Who washed the disciple's feet that night,
And said, 'Now wash each others for this is right?'
Who prayed so hard in the Garden of Gethsemane,
And said to those with him, 'Keep watch here for me?'
Who was betrayed by a kiss from a friend,
And knew that His life was reaching it's end?

Who was on trial and beaten so cruel,
A crown of thorns on his head, but without any jewel?
Who was the one as the cook crowed twice,
Was denied by Peter, not one but thrice?
Who was found guilty and yet innocent,
Suffering in pain, his body so bent?
Who took the place of a murderer there,
And who was the one that made them all stare?
Who was relieved of His cross to Golgotha,
Being followed by women including His mother?
Whose garments did they then cast by lot,
And as he was hanging knew of their plot?
Who caused the darkness to cover the land, And knew all along what his Father had planned?
Whose was the one, the ultimate sacrifice,
And said to the thief, 'Today you'll be with me in paradise?'
Who then in anguish and complete agony,
Cried, 'My God, my God, why hast thou forsaken me?'
Who said as He was dying, 'Father forgive,'
And paid the price so that sinners can live?
Who said, 'It is finished,' and gave up His spirit,
And who is the one who deserves all the credit?
Whose death then tore the temple curtain in two,
Caused the earthquake and opened the saints' graves there too?
Who was then begged for, His body so scarred,
And sealed in a tomb, with soldiers on guard?
Whose tomb was found empty, the stone rolled away,
Who rose from the dead on the very third day?
Who appeared to Mary and said, 'Go tell them it's me,'
And that they will see me in Galilee?'
Who said to them all, 'I will leave you never,
I am with you always, now and forever?'
Who is the one of all this is true?
The Lord Jesus Christ, that is who.

Teresa Mary Street

TRUSTY

I flay your skin to save mine own,
For I am the trusty and you're going down.

I am the bailiff, nineteen stone
Of beef, bone and muscle, no fat
And no brain, suited, booted
Through your door, into your life
Nice telly, mate, I'll take that
I like her too: nice wife.

I flay your skin to save mine own,
For I am the trusty and you're going down.

I am the copper, leery and mean
You're an easy collar; look guilty to me
Targets, tea breaks and no heart
Lock you up, let you sweat
Got any drugs, mate? Like some?
Nah, only joking, you're nicked.

I flay your skin to save mine own,
For I am the trusty and you're going down.

I am the social worker, nobody's friend
Lead a decent, innocent life
But I'll get you in the end
Lies, targets and more lies
Skewer you on my twisted reality
For I am God.

I flay your skin to save mine own,
For I am the trusty and you're going down.

You the reader: middle class, well off,
Respectable, surely not?
Exaggeration, hysteria, can't be true,
Surely not the boys in blue
Then there's a knock on the door
And they've come for you.

The pagan gods are hungry, the trusty's safe
You're the human sacrifice and it's too late.

Paul Corcoran

ESCAPE

There is a place to where I go,
It's close down by the sea.
And through a gate I often pass,
That's only known to me.

The sights and sounds I see here,
Are wondrous to behold,
And I am there amongst these views,
The marvels in my mind unfold.
The Taj Mahal and Grand Canyon,
Are here for me to see.
The Polar Caps, Niagra Falls,
Appear as if for me.

The Burmese Temples spring from
Jungles verdant green,
The dusty Indian market with their
Smells of spices and aromas,
Appear upon the scene.

I cross the great Sahara in a camel caravan,
And sleep at night in a Bedouin tent.
I boat along the Amazon and marvel at the sight.
And I am breathless with the Northern Lights,
On a dark Norwegian night.

I view the world from Everest's Peak,
And walk the Great China Wall.
I round Cape Horn and fight mountainous seas,
Before I reach calm water.
It's time now to set a course for home,
My adventure now is over.

Oh! So your back at last.
I swear you'll walk the legs of that poor dog.
Your dinner's in the oven,
Though I doubt it's fit to eat.
The lawns need cutting and the hedges could do with a trim.
I'm just popping over to see Mother.
Yes Dear, give her my love.

Patrick John Conroy

THE SUDDEN SMELL OF BURNING WOOD

Seeing the moon in the day
And old cracked willows that sway.
Eating ripe figs and not feeling bilious,
Plus the palest of skies like those of Ravillious.

Feeling the happy sense of a special grace
And friends with a vicar who believes in God's grace,
That's confirmed by my girl with that smile on her face,
Who, (like the sudden smell of burning wood) makes me feel good.

The joy of wireless and on Radio Four
I listen to cricket not knowing the score –
Yes that's me, calm as a dove and like the snake wily,
So getting away with the sweet life of Riley.

And lighting a candle, not cursing the dark,
I face the world with an open heart,
While knowing a love that's always the same,
Having nothing to lose and so much to gain.

Huw Parsons

SOME OTHER TIME

What now that love creates
Amongst those undercurrents relate
Oh bitter-sweet divine and great
Such harvest brings plums, grapes
Old schoolboy modest reflects
Upon the mystery souls all gone
Eye of needle Bible book, bell, candle
And plenty more cannot get a handle
Wild idea of famous fable told
And what if I on shaky promise
Close illusions broom and proper
Seek perfection, never mind venture
Oh and roots and class will banter
In final hour such questions matter
Against the flow of toil and slaughter
Such rolling sea and summer breeze
And the well of cool spring water
Look back and forward sleeping sun

Malachy Trainor

THROUGH YOUR WINDOW

Through your window I see a brook,
So now is the time to write a poem for my book.
The morning sun is hot and bright
And warms the paper as I write.
Frogs and grasshoppers cross the path,
As they jump they make me laugh.

Ducks and swans float on by
And leaping fish catch my eye.
Baby cygnets follow their mother,
Flap their wings and splash each other.
Reeds and water lilies flourish six months of the year
And otters and seagulls are always here.

The water laps the rugged bank
And washes lilies off a rotting plank,
Baby cygnets give chase,
But their mother is quick to slow their pace.
I open your window, inhale the fresh air
And smell fragrance of flowers everywhere.

Some people stop and say hello
As an otter swims by very slow.
I stop and speak for a little while
Then bid them farewell, with a gentle smile.

I must finish this poem by the end of the day,
The animals have inspired me, in a poetic sort of way.

David John Hewett

MY DOG SNOOPY

I brought this puppy off my friend,
Whose name is Wend,
I got told,
He's about nine weeks old.

He's quite small and fat
And it looks like a rat.
He is black and brown
And loves to spin around.
He even slides on his belly like a snail
And loves to chase his little waggling tail.

I take him out to the park
And all he does is *bark! Bark! Bark!*
Maybe he likes the sound of his bark you see!

He eats his meat, off his feet
And it really cannot be? But, but,
He likes drinking tea.

He also has a favourite game,
Called chase the shoe lace,
Before he lays his little head,
Down for bed.

Now I've decided to call my dog Snoopy!
'Cause he is rather loopy.
Oh well!
My dog Snoopy is always gonna be my best friend
Until the end!

Rita Golding

VERTIGO

If
You
Can
Say
You
Can,
Without
The use of
Blindfolds,
Climb to the
Top of the
Tangled ironworks
Of the Eiffel Tower
Faster than the lifts
And not break out into
A sweat with your eyes
Open and breathing easily
And then stop and look
Down and view the Seine –
You have a head for heights

Or
If you
Can claim
Your pod
And head
For the
Stars and
Sway and
Revolve while
Swinging gently
As the
London Wheel
Climbs and
Descends
And then stop and view the Thames –
You have a head for heights

Me . . . I have vertigo . . . and I go green.

Robert Main

LOVE IS . . .

Love is a question,
A wondering, doubting sudden shaft of light
An awareness, small and laughing,
Swallowed in the clamour and the noise . . .
A quaint illusion.

Love is a dreading,
A frightened, shuddering of confused and worried thought,
A nightmare thing to flee and to cast away!
Yet running, comfort and a glow inside,
A shadow in the soul.

Love is a challenge –
As unexpected as the sun in winter
And as unpredictable –
A boisterous, optimist – carefree and capricious,
A demon extrovert.

Love is a silent thing –
A lonely world of cold interpretation
An agony of conjecture, of weighing thoughts and glances
Of balancing unspoken theories –
The ambiguity of wordless comment.

Love is loyally and coming off the fence
An utter single-minded unity of thought and purpose,
A wiling and entire monopoly,
A star, a two-way oneness.

Love is an arc of music –
Incessant calling of a siren violin –
A nodding of the flower drums –
A movement imperceptible –
A rhythm in the bones.

Love is an army, inevitable in its purpose,
The trampling, stabbing white hot pain of want
The pulsing, beating throbbing of achievement
The tumultuous ebb flow of battle joined
The choking mastery of a victory won
A gentle violence.

Love is a quiet thing
The tenderness of sweet acceptance
And the peace of giving.
Serenity, a contented lull –
A compromise, a whispered prayer –
The answer.

Jane Brooks

SWEEPY

Although your going away
was very sad, in a way
I'm happy to say
I saw you today
before you drifted so gently to sleep.

As I stroked and patted you Sweep,
I said, 'Goodbye sweetheart,
and, thank you for the sweet part
you played in my life, visiting me,
this neighbour, and, being so free
with your loving affection,
and, true heart. Your furry (purr) fection
will remain with me a long spiritual time, like a favourite song –
gently haunting!

You leave a hole in your mum's life, a sorrowful space,
as loved pets do. For, you all lace
our existences with genuine love
which emanates from Heaven above,
for, there is no pretence in any of you,
only truth and sense, found in very few
human beings!

Bye-bye Sweep –
be happy,
rest, enjoy your sleep.

St Francis bless.

Mhairi Jarvis

FROM A SCHOOL PHILOSOPHY 1968

Who am I?

A little child with a life to live
Who needs the 'food' that is yours to give,
With time to learn and laugh and play
In mine own unique individual way;
With time to do and time to rest
Then time to rise on another crest;
With time to 'paddle' and then to 'swim',
So, when a teenager, I can really 'dive in'.

Teach me to read and help me to write
A little each day – bite after bite;
Help me to listen to what I am told
And to talk and speak clearly – happily bold;
Stories, I love to hear, books to look through,
Turning the pages enthralls me anew;
Songs to sing and poems to recite
Making me want to read, draw and write
Well structured with spellings I learn to be right.

Let counting be fun and make it a game
So that numbers are meaningful and not just a name;
Let me learn 'sums' in a practical way
Doing and recording, a little each day.
Making number patterns with counters or bricks
Adding and subtracting and sharing out tricks.
Shopping with money, buying and giving change,
So much to learn in a vast learning range.
Shapes and sizes to make and measure
Learning by doing is always a pleasure.
Tables I'll learn will be well understood
Recited by rote and remembered for good
And I'll do sums in my head when I am grown up!

I need to run and jump and play ball,
Have adventures, outdoor activities and explore,
Be creative with my mind and hands
And have make-belief play in boy/girl bands.

Give me a chance to be myself – me –
In my mind and being, as busy as a bee;
Storing up knowledge I'm making mine own
The outcome of which I shall one day make known.

Thus, so I learn from the time I was born –
A baby, a toddler, years one, two, three and four.

But please remember I am only five
And after another year I shall only be six
And going on to seven is no quick fix.

Who am I?
A little child with a life to live
Who needs the 'food' that is yours to give.
Let me dance and sing and laugh with joy,
A happy girl – learning – a happy boy.

Agnes Hickling

OTHER PEOPLE'S WAR

As daylight dimmed into night
The bombardment began,
A baptism into war for the innocents,
Dipped in dismay, each and every man.

A barrage of noise breaks up the land
Hour after long hour,
Fear galloped in gullets and down into dirt,
Tongues thick, yellow and sour.

They wept at the carnage collapsed around,
What sacrifices hung in red shreds
On the altar of someone else's war,
Given as blessings bestowed on all their heads.

Some were sent ahead to scout about,
A hidden sniper's bullet seared the air
Body dropped, dust flew from charred rags,
Into the sun's early morning glare.

Mars hung raw in the strangely quiet dawn,
Out of the haze a bird's solo song
Seemed out of place. Dante's inferno over,
Fireworks of the night now gone.

Day is filled with troops on the move with
Ammunition and longed-for letters to be read,
Amongst the debris, lie boots and limbs of
Soldier and child alike, all of them dead.

Sandy Phillips

INMATES

There's no escape!

We're unwarranted prisoners of your illness,
And we find ourselves captive; totally confined.
All thoughts of taking part in conversation gone,
As further back into your withered shell you crawl.

There's no escape!

While the weeks pass; seasons change but we fail to see,
In our dim house we remain incarcerated.
We both stare outside as healthy people walk by,
Lucky! They don't lie in their bed and hear you cry.

For both of us there's no escape.

Susan Mullinger

REMINISCING

Having been born in the year of three kings
During my life I have seen many things
Lived through the terrors of being at war
When we dreaded the knock of the postman on the door
Witnessed the crowning of Elizabeth, our Queen
Never before such splendour been seen
Stood in wonder at eclipse of the sun
Here in my lifetime millennium
I have lived through recession
Counting the cost
Standing together so not all was lost
Now here I am and it's Jubilee
The splendour once more, a big family
I guess there is always a silver lining
To show us the way when things are declining
Once more look forward with hope in our hearts
Not let depression tear us apart.

Audrey Allocca

WHEN WILL IT END?

On the bloodstained sands
A beggar slept, his bowl beside him lay,
No passer-by will view his plight
Or a pitied sigh display.

In war-torn ruins, urchins play
Searching amongst the dust,
A cripple at the roadside pleads
For water and a crust.

Young mothers cry their silent tears
Beside a smouldering pyre,
Deep sorrows burden now their souls
Their life without desire.

On the bloodstained sands
A beggar sleeps, a smile upon his face,
For in his dreams, a widow's mite
Inside his bowl is placed.

Malcolm Wilson Bucknall

DARKEST HOURS

When the evening falls
Will you say my name, think of me?
Starlight, moon bright, cool whispering breeze,
Owl cries.
As the rest of the world sleeps, why can't I?
Eyes shut tight . . .
Moonlight shines on down through the night
Casting soft shadows in the bright, white and silver light . . .
Illuminating the trees, gently following the luminous streams . . .
Memories still cloud my thoughts . . .
I can't stop the horror of losing you from haunting me once more,
My heart cries out in pain
Then, I hear you softly say my name . . .
Soothing, calming, I close my eyes once more,
Blessed sleep reclaims me.
Come and stay with me, and let me find your love again,
In a place where angels sing out your name.

N Brocks

THE JURASSIC CURRAGHS!

Walking into the Curraghs
On a blustery cloudy day,
The atmosphere was very still
No sunshine on this Saturday,
As we started walking
The clouds darkened
The rain started – pouring
Decision taken – back to the car!
Disappointed, driving down the lane
We find another parking space
Hurrah! The sun comes out again,
Going through the trees
Gnarled and twisted – no leaves,
An atmospheric aura pervades
We go into a Jurassic clime
Part mangrove swamp – creepily
The silence absorbs us
Who knows what is lurking
Hoping to see wild wallabies
But it wasn't meant to be.
Finally the icing on the cake
Weather change again
A snowy blizzard engulfs us
It seems like climate change.

Elizabeth Adams

SOMETHING FAINT AND FAR AWAY

Something faint and far away
- Something I loved.

'Did you – do you exist in reality?'
I ask the fleeting dream or long-past memory.
'I did – I do.'
A recent dream is so like something in the past
- The long past.

The struggle to remember is the same.
Sometimes, something stands out,
But this one is
So faint and far away
And yet so poignant.
Is it from my childhood home?
Or longer past?
Or Heaven?

Something faint and far away
- Something I loved.

Jacqueline Ward

ARABIA

Asked to stay forever
In this neck of the woods
Stood firm upon the ground
Overcome all weakness
Day by day
Make a big deal
Work like never before
Shed a little light
On the situation here
Arabia, gather all in
Include the top set
Arabia – 'Newman of the Year' selection completed!

S M Thompson

SAYING GOODBYE TO FRANK

It was from the ferry,
Proud boat of the Mersey
That in one way
We gained closure for emotions
But could not for memories.
They cannot be taken away
Until we are no longer here
To have them.
To share them
We will remember them for you.

As the shards of grey ash
All we had left of you
Whirled away and down
Into the mighty river
Powering past
You went home
And we cried, 'Goodbye Frank!
You were a special person.'

Goodbye, Frank.

Christine Kennett

GRIEF

I think I hear your footstep on the stair
Although I know it cannot be
I run to see

I think I see your face among the crowd
Although I know I am mistook
I stop and look

I think I hear your voice
About the house
Although I know you sleep
Within your tomb
I search each room

Why? When reason tells me
This is all in vain
Because you were and always will be
A part of me.

E Urmston

LEFT ON THE SHELF

A lonely shoe sat on a shelf
Sighing, 'Why must I be by myself?'
A left shoe that's left alone
'No Mr Right to call my own

I need to be part of a pair
I need a sole-mate who can share
The way I think, the way I feel
When I'm feeling down at heel

I'd like to meet him face to face
I'd invite him to undo my lace
My tongue is singing like a linnet
Till someone puts their foot right in it

We'd make such a perfect pair
Side by side beneath the chair
And we'd dance a reel and rock and roll
Lace and heel, sock and sole'

Sandra Miles

SANTA'S LITTLE HELPER

Beggars aren't hungry but we still just say no to drugs.
Hate thugs and incarcerate the innocent.
Far from a penny,
Where I'm from there's many.
Nothing new, how it was lucky for some of the few.
None for the rest.
It was going to be a long night.
I could look down to a kite.
Wished we were all on the save level like power and energy.
But that's enough of me.
It's just a thought.
Guilty was only a verdict read out in court.
I'm still on the road.
Now tell me why it has to turn?
Parts were missing like years spent in prison.
You picked the wrong day because I died that night.
I still wasn't an angel.
They made gambling legal.
Played to win whatever kind a world we lived in.

Aaron Noel

PAUPER'S LAMENT

Through the sweat and the grime
just a meaning, no end
a test of resolve
for the portrait you paint
a lifetime's appraisal never to reap
show no mercy till the weary sleep

Day after day turns year into years
the wheels keep turning
while the oil runs dry
don't bleat or complain
you're not even sheep
just a name and a number on somebody's sheet

Wind weather the storm
no grace or lucidity
a modern day peasant
from typecast terrain
life's for who dares not for who cares
an uphill climb for the want of your wares

Suffer in silence
your toils what they need
in all that surrounds
and what's thrown at your feet
the struggle and worry in poverty rife
an age old manuscript carried through life

Beggar man, worker man
a creation through time
no sentiment spared or step out from behind
just contempt with the blame
always challenged at will
then left in the gutter holding the bill

A penance you pay on the way to the grave
earning your poverty
with little to spare
never a refund, the glass always empty
left with nothing
from this world full of plenty

Paul Nicholson

THE ENGLISH RIVIERA

I travelled on holiday
To Devon by the sea,
Torquay, Paignton, Brixton,
The south coast to see.

Rows of hotels,
I booked into my room,
I had my evening meal,
It was fresh and cool.

We walked to the sea front,
The ocean was blue,
Across the other side,
Houses all in view.

Yachts of every kind,
Oared in the harbour.
Palm trees everywhere,
Seagulls flying higher.

I visited Paignton,
All the shops to see,
A wonderful holiday,
Enjoyable for me.

Certainly an experience,
Somewhere that I have never been.
I would love to return,
The English Riviera to see.

Carol Jean Beart

FIRST LOVE

This is the story of Molly Keen,
Who had the blondest hair you've ever seen,
She was the prettiest girl I'd ever saw,
The day she moved in next door,

She had some freckles just one or two
And her eyes were the deepest colour blue,
I walked her to school on her first day,
She held my hand part of the way,

At the door I saw a tear,
I smiled and whispered, 'I'm always here,'
And at the bell at half-past three,
She ran and threw her arms around me,

'To settle into a school so new,'
She said, 'I sat all day and thought of you,'
From that day her heart was mine,
I'd fallen in love at the age of nine,

We laughed and played and just hung out,
Because that's what friends is all about,
But as one day we walked, her hand in mine,
Outside her house we saw a sign,

On a post with a rusty nail,
In big red letters it said: For Sale,
Both sets of parents looked so glum,
But we were unprepared at the news to come,

We both cried tears that fell to the floor,
When we realised we would see each other no more,
The house was sold and she moved away,
I really think it was my saddest day,

An old man with his dog now lives there in the dark,
The curtains stay drawn, which makes the dog bark,
I often think of Molly Keen,
And ponder at what might have been,

Even now it's hard to understand when,
You lose your girlfriend at the age of ten,
Although I'm an old man, my, heavens above,
It still really hurts when you lose your first love.

Bazil Figura

POETRY

Poetry is a load of crap,
Don't bother me, you stupid sap,
I don't want any of your opinions,
Save them for some other minions,
I hate Keats and I hate Byron,
So let's not have a bloomin' try on!

Fine my friend if that's how you feel,
But how about we do a deal?
Shall we have you whisht your noise,
And I will chat to these girls and boys.
If verse is a constipation devoutly to be missed,
Then what about if I insist
That a pop song, my dear old prune,
Is a poem that someone has given a tune.

From 'Auld Lang Syne' to 'Land of Hope and Glory',
From 'Jerusalem' to 'Tell Me the Old Story',
From 'Delilah' to the 'Saints Go Marching in',
It's a poem if you take out all the din,
Or music as some people call it,
The tune that makes it into a hit,
Just write me a pop song and don't go hysteric,
You simple are going to need a lyric,
Here's your chance, what I think will come next
Is a song with a lyric that's written in text.

Martin Levy

AND MONEY'S ANOTHER

'Something to ask, Mr Peterbro;
You mustn't think that I'm mad . . .
Would you mind – I mean – I just wonder . . .'

'Nay, of course you can, my lad!
You can have her, and may you both prosper!'

Jack frowns, and says, 'Well - but have who?'

'Why, aren't we discussing my daughter?
You're wanting to marry our Prue?'

Young man found his throat had dried up;
He swallowed but made little sound.
Then – 'You misunderstood, Mr Peterbro:
I'm wanting a loan – fifty pound!'

Pa ponders, stares hard and then splutters:
'He's turned down our Prue! Well, blow me!
And as for borrowing five tenners . . .
Nay lad, truth is – I scarce know thee!'

Howard Peach

BUTTERFLY CINQUAIN

Who knows
What others know.
What others know of you!
They know as much as you reveal,
and feel.
It may be something that you sense,
Your senses in defence.
Big deal!

Robin Martin-Oliver

OUR HIGHLAND QUEEN

Morning mist surrounds the mountains
Clinging to rocks and the trees
Crags and gullies, glens and cairns
A mystical sight to see
Hear a hundred pipers playing
Crossing the hills and the streams
They are making their way to share the day
With our beautiful Highland Queen.

All over the land, the great chiefs of the clans
With their people go many a mile
For our future Queen she has never been seen
By the Highlanders marching in style
The heather is purpled, and bracken is trampled
With rowan tree leaves turning brown
The site is being set for this wondrous event
Our first Highland Queen to be crowned.

As well as MacDonald of Sleet and clan Ranald
There's Lewis and Harris Macleod
From Gordon and Farquharson westward to Cameron
To this highland coronation they're bound
Where there's music, romancing, singing and dancing
To strathspeys and reels swirling round
They are travelling far from Barra and Mar
To see Our Highland Queen – with her crown.

Hunter Buchanan

DEPARTURE

I was a volcano
Staggering through early morning fog
cold cobwebs of confusion lurking
My knife-edged tongue was sharp
It stung you like a demented bee
pride prevailed; worried words wrecked
exits through slammed door
cobwebs of confusion clouded
dismissing dreams of 'Have a nice day!'
I was rain falling in a veil off tears
I was a sky several shades of charcoal
A twisted tornado

I reasoned – stopped dead in my tracks
knowing there was still time
you would still be there
you were a wounded wolf
No! I had a train to catch in the rain
But I would phone you . . . later . . .
heart racing I was chasing great shadows

I was a fox on the run
and where was the summer sun?
June's rapid rain
'midst miserable gushing rush-hour
the constant honk of traffic cacophony yelling in my ears
tyres hissed, rain pissed (or kissed)

I checked my watch
a train in the rain . . .
why had we argued?
Suddenly a short, sharp pang
My mobile rang. I fell knowing
You would never hear my apology!

Judy Studd

THANK YOU GIRLS

I have six lovely granddaughters
Amy, Katie, Lucy, Chloe, Sophie and Hannah
They all mean the world to me
And are very helpful to their nana

Whenever we are together
They brighten up my day
And really make me chuckle
At the priceless things they say

They once asked if I was a little girl
When the dinosaurs were here
My answer to that question was
I just missed them by a couple of years

Over the years they have given me drawings
Cards and letters too
Little poems and stories
So thanks to all of you

All these things I will keep for ever
I love you all so much
You really are six smashers
I think you're *fabulous.*

Jackie Richardson

OLD AGE

I write to keep young,
drink moonshine each day.
Go shooting and fishing
with a starboard list sway.
I like gardening and caravanning
and live like a redskin,
lie out in the sunshine
while the stills bubbling.
I just take it easy,
for I have worked all my life,
I do what I want to,
to hell with the wife.
You could say I'm selfish
perhaps that's what I am,
but I ain't old and miserable
I can still hold a can.
But when I'm departed,
I shall rise out the ground,
and go shooting and poaching,
around the churchyard compound.

John Hickman

RELAY

Our days run at different times,
But, on parallel lines.

Where you see beauty,
I argue monotony.

The night to share these plates, drinks and sights,
Is lost to the morning.

We were never written onto one page.

Lucy Jordan

LIAISON

I wait for you all afternoon,
My flesh is moist with sweat.
Silk sheets crease beneath me,
But what I want, I can't have yet.

You slowly slide in close to me,
Our limbs are intertwined,
And though I cannot say the words,
Ours is a love divine.

My skin ignites with perfect lust
And all my fears, I shed.
And as we writhe, a voice exclaims,
'Oi! Get off that bed!'

Though young love's a splendid thing,
Context is all, I fear.
Perhaps meeting in John Lewis
Was not the best idea.

Leanne Moden

UNICORNS CARE

I took the stitches out after four days instead of the suggested ten,
Was fairly confident of my steady hand and the nib of my fountain pen,
Home surgery with odd unsterilised tools may sound a little perverse,
As the last thread slid out it opened up like a Venus Flytrap in reverse,
Out came a stream of crimson and a double rainbow, a pot of gold too,
And a sad little unicorn walked up my arm and handed me some superglue.

Havana Jaques

FOR WHAT WE GOT WRONG

For what we got wrong
they won't forgive us
The young we have failed
they inherit our sins
and charges will follow . . .
That we fostered self-disrespect
and willfully worshipped false gods
refused to recognise evil
lost the will to punish the criminal
and allowed monsters to flourish
That we let our children down
educated them in ignorance
and instructed them by neglect
Abandoned the old and the ill
and left the poor to rot
Tolerated politicians
feathering their nests
while telling us 'This
is as good as it gets!'
That we let ourselves be ruled
by bleeding liberal hearts
those metropolitan musers –
hypocrites by instinct
tired old political tarts

That we sent soldiers to die
to fight an imperfect cause
while those with so much
blood on their hands
(the instigators, of course)
got their thirty pieces of silver
and walked away from their wars

For what we got wrong
they won't forgive us
In our dotage we'll be
dragged to The Hague
and tried for our crimes
against common sense
our memories
conveniently vague
We wanted to die
before we got old –
no bloody wonder
no one will miss us

when we're all
six feet under

For what we got wrong
they won't forgive us
and why should they?
I tell myself it's not my fault
I didn't screw the nation
but still my guilt becomes me
by age and association

Steve Greenhalgh

IDIOT CHILDREN

We know it's true because they told us so . . .
There is no need, therefore, to question
books, that false-strewn with hear-a-say, unfold
despicable and sickly greed-spoused debt to blood redemption

We fear the wrath because they told us so . . .
Faith cowed, the blighted scope of reason
looks not wonder-eyed to humbling hubbled-heaven's design,
lest for to cite an intelligence of treason

We share the blame because they said we must . . .
Stain immemorial, so consciously ordained
and ingrained as guilt, such original and lustful phallusy,
repressed by those so sense-undressed and logic-maimed

We bear the yoke still now of power-manufactured trust
But now, the fairy-stale of infantile approbations
must be fiction, cringe-consigned to purile nascene
Truth belies belief in unkind childish consolations

God is not great, you idiot children
Allow your spirit not such tainted limitation
Hitch-up the curtains of enlightenment
Uncover and deny all false prostration

Neil Benton

AN EMPIRE AND ALL THIS WASHING

An empire and all this washing
Piled up like battlements on
The kitchen worktop. Balled iron
Socks thud into bedding;
Coughed from the cannons of my feet.
I have defended our city since you left,
The besieged streets now littered
With packets of casualty crisps. I am
The emperor of empty cans
And food packaging, filling the gaps
Between now and then

You and me

My ascension announced by
A fanfare of litter and
A thousand bitter cups of tea.
I hold the single ruling seat
My badge of office a sour
Downturned mouth,
Not the one you wrapped
Your lips around.

Frederic John Greenall

MILAGE

The fiery angel said:
'Retrieve the load you left
Lying there upon the track
And bear it on your back.
It is yourself, your life
To use and give away.
Carry it with a song:
The journey is not long.'

Josephine Thompson

FOR ME

Sitting at my desk, waiting for inspiration.
Spending time doodling along, that's when my mind starts to sing its song.

The words appear like a magic show, and then off I go.
Scribbling so quickly and precise, the words falling like confetti grains of rice.

Over the paper my pen makes its way and my mind is now running far away.
Words about this and that and sometimes nothing at all.

One day when you're far away, one day when you're home in bed.
One day when you feel you're dead, one day when you're happy instead.

Poems are personal to the person themselves,
And my poems come along like a bunch of little elves.

I always seem to have time to put my pen to paper and see what it will bring.
I like it when it happens, it makes my heart sing.

I feel at ease when I write the words, I feel at peace with my inner world.
I feel chillaxed and nothing can stop me. I like to write my poems for all to see.
But most importantly I write them for me.

Julie Gibbon

BROKEN

The storm that passed spread out its wings
And created a circle of such devastating things.
It wove its way around your path,
Crashed its fingers and stole your laugh.
It wrapped up your love and threw it aside,
Encased it in rain along with your pride.
It stole your sun and left you grey,
Pinned down your hopes and left you astray.
The clouds burst in and cut your heart,
Pulled out your feelings and ripped them apart.
It tried to destroy you,
Turn your kindness to stone and went so fast, leaving you all alone.
Threatened in darkness, and clung to cold walls,
Wake up the little angels and wait for their calls.
Let them bring back pure skies and love all abound.
Let them lift up your heart and hear its healing sound.
Let the grass feel cool under the caress of your hand
And the gentle breeze mend your thoughts in the glowing sand.

Vivienne Gill

THE HAPPY COUPLE

My long-time friend for all my life
And thank you to his blushing bride
This means so much the words flow out
Taking a second with you all now
How close can two people be?
Everything is here for you all to see
When all today is done
All families will come
Now together as one
Don't go away, the fun is to stay and help the happy couple celebrate
Really quite proud to know
Everything does show
Be happy forever love can only grow
Every time you look at this I want you to know
Can't put into words how much it means
'Cause for people to know it's all their dreams
Always know this, I feel proud to know you both and your families now

Peter Piwowarski

RELICT OF THE ABOVE

They have taken the bones from St Andrew's yard
They have taken the bones away.
The hallowed remains of burgesses
Were spirited out today.
Properly incised on memorial stone
The following text appeared;-
William Thomas, Merchant in wine.
Anne – relict of the above, died
In seventeen hundred and twenty-nine.

Did you hear her voice which cried
Echoing down the years?
Bring them back, bring them back
These poor scraps you cast away my dears.
These poor scraps are human bones
Relict of Anne Thomas.

Gerry Wheatley

COPING WITH NEUROLOGICAL ILLNESS

(Dedicated to my neurologist, Dr Myles Connor)

My whole body aches though I smile through the pain
Some days I find it helps if I stand out in the rain.
I walk, talk about the everyday things that life brings.

Birthdays, Christmas, church events
It prevents the sadness getting in.
I walk with a walking stick now
Before I use to run

Jump

Shout

Or just fool about.

No longer can I cycle

Or dance or juggle

No I am not a

muggle, I am a mud blood.

I can't do this or that when I want
Like I used to do.
'Help!' I scream inside my head
But no one can hear but me.
No one can hear the fear I feel when limbs go numb.
In the middle of the night I wake to no feeling in my arms and legs.
My tremors and shakes get me annoyed
I am also unemployed
'Help! Help! Help!'
I scream
Inside this nightmare dream
I wake to the sound of my own scream.

Elizabeth Phillips Scott

SILVER SCREEN

I feel like the end of a movie.
Credits stretched,
with VHS skips
and the memory of a story all cut up in bits
where I was not the hero.
And the names flash past
too fast to grasp,
with mad dash for the door,
with a solemn
chord
held on a piano.
I waited.
For the lives of the people up on the big screen
To change into nightmares from what once were dreams
where I, a minor character,
played a major role in bringing
everything together.

But the music still lingers.
And I'm still sat biting my fingers
Waiting . . .
For the woman I loved
to wake up and realise
this man is not right for her.
And she is not right for this man.
Happily ever after has to have an end,
and considering I was a catalyst
whose wounds won't mend,
I feel obliged to change their lives –
I feel my heart capsize
in my chest,
taking deep breaths
as I looked the other way,
only ever once wishing death
and not in that way –
I wished death on myself.

As I stood there in silence
I bundled my thoughts,
holding onto memories that I knew were yours
from a different perspective.
You had seasons
in your soul.
And mine
is lined with gold.

And I'm waiting in the dark for the credits to end,
my mind full of messages too anguished to send,
rewinding the scenes when we were still friends
and waiting.

For the reel to catch fire
and burn through our lives
erasing my grief.
As the end of the spool
spins out of control
I realise –
I am not the end of the movie.
These feelings.
These thoughts.
This lust.
This nonsense.
Distrust.
The horror inside
that eats through my mind
are all very much present

with what I left behind.
It's dark.
And that's how my days will be spent –
Sat in the dark,
remembering what it was like to be friends.
And waiting to see how happily ever after ends.

Edward Christopher Watts

IN TRANSIT . . .

The plume of ash
Spewing across the network morning news
Flashes,
Flickering,
On hotel TV.
Doomed to another day of Beijing smog
Invading the fifteenth floor window,
Open in the stifling heat
No air-conditioning allowed till May
They say
Bored by events so far away, (to them mundane)
And shaken by
Yushu's deadly quake:
Two thousand dead, and rising . . .

Volcano's grim gash of lava
Grounds great kites of steel.
No cash can contain this
No sash of silk, glimmering gold
In red lantern's light
Can cocoon us from
The forbidden thought
That in this city,
Behind the great wall of Earth's indifference,
Lost from family's fold
And fellowship of friends – not clichés now,
Imprisoned by a dragon's fire
Five thousand miles away
We are flotsam
Ice and ash
Yin and yang.

Jane Coundley

WHAT IS LOVE WITHOUT WORDS

Don't wait for me to come,
I am always around.
I drift away but I still care,
We never quite made it but the connection was there.
I would sail the oceans twice over again,
If it lead me to knowledge of how to be close to you, my friend,
And you would fight for queen and country,
Because you'd know you would be protecting me once more.
But alas, we made no such move,
Time stood still upon the things we once stood for.
A kick-start is needed to get it roaring once more.

A tattoo on my heart still shows,
A declaration of love never fades,
Silently sighing, simmering in intention,
A purpose of which one's blood does sing,
As it passes my heart, reading the words
I still remember, just a dream of the past
Where our hands never touched,
But our minds did explore
Words of significance,
And feelings you see,
As what is love without words,
And words without love?

Sophie Banks

CHOICES

A road I had not travelled, how hard could that walk be?
Others will have gone before and cleared a path for me.
I'm not a special person, why should I have a choice?
The road for me is chosen . . . and then I heard a little voice!

'Grandma, I need you with me, we have so much to do!
You need to show me lots of things . . . I have to learn from you!
I need to go to school yet and show you what I've done.
I want to laugh and play with you; you're going to have such fun!
My sister's just a baby; don't you want to see her smile?
To cuddle her and kiss her, cos girls like that (for a while)
She has to learn to walk yet, wear pigtails in her hair.
Don't you want to help her learn to talk? Please Grandma don't go there . . .'

A road I had not travelled, how hard could that walk be?
At the end of it, my daughter would be waiting there you'll see!
Her smiling face, her open arms, my heart was torn in two.
The road for me is chosen . . . then my daughter's voice came through.

'Mum, I need you with me, there's so much we didn't do!
But I can see my sister's children need you just as much, can't you?
Go help them learn to live a life that's fun and full of joy,
A pretty little princess and such a loving little boy!
I had eleven happy years and I treasured every minute
But their lives will be far richer for having you, Mum, in it.'

A road I've yet to travel, I'll take that walk some other time.
Be there my darling daughter to help me make that climb.
Little hands are gently pulling me from this unfamiliar track . . .
'We love you Grandma, stay with us . . . until Jesus calls you back.'

Lesley Elaine Greenwood

A BELL THAT RINGS AND WAKES

Follow my mind – let me take you some place,
behind my eyes,
where you're sure to find a story,
where today's truth lies.
Trust me, when I hold out my hand,
In the hope that I can guide you,
through the would-be sheets of paper and the pounding turned up loud.
Let me show you my every day,
laid open and exposed for you to understand,
to map the way from flowers to heaving pain,
for you to trace,
each undetected hiccup in every hundred breaths.

I wish I could draw – in pastels –
or sing and it to sound like the intention,
but, inner-self betrayed,
all attempts to sound a shiver,
A bell that rings and wakes,
wet with tears.

I cannot offer you beauty, I can't offer you notes practiced and fine-tuned –
but let me offer you a journey,
a truth,
painfully real,
that might help you fall in love with where I started,
beautifully plain,
let you glimpse a sight of before we parted,
let you see yourself a soul that uncorrupted,
is yours and all I hoped to be.

Talisa Dean

FIVE YEARS NOW

Tanya, May 12th, we have known each other, for five years

Sometimes I am angry at you, and my eyes fill with tears!
You always promise and say things, but never do . . .
Then you say something, I want to hear, and I have to say, 'I love you!'

I hate it when you send me mail, and I never get . . .
One is OK but more is odd, which makes me upset!
Did you really post it, I ask?
If you really love me, you would do this simple task!

This year (2012), on 29th Feb, you asked to 'marry you'
I joked you should, but it be nice, if this was true!
Maybe you can ask again, if you want, on one knee . . .
Perhaps in an Indian port, in Puri!

Looking back on emails all these year(s),
I asked you the same questions, which I want to hear . . .
'Christmas/New Year, meet your family, see me more . . .
Two weeks not hours, unless I am a bore?'

Three years ago, there was a 'very slight hiccup',
Your love went downhill, but please, let it go, all the way, up?
I would love to be with you for a 1000 year(s),
So we could have loads of parties, and I will cheer!

Barry Ryan

JUST CALLED HATS

A bowler, is a hat to put on your head,
A nightcap, that you might wear in bed,
A boater perhaps to wear on a lake,
Now a cook's hat, just to aid you to bake.

At a wedding, he'd wear a top hat,
The bride, well she'd look better than that,
With veil gently caressing her face,
So delicate, and surrounded by lace.

A babe's woolly bonnet, so snug and warm,
To a baby girl, it adds to her charm,
Now a baseball cap, must be back to front,
In black or red, whatever you want.

A beret is smart, if turned to the side,
Just right for shopping, if you've a mind,
A busby, a problem – too heavy to wear,
To stand for the Queen, while others stare.

A milliner's a name for one who makes hats,
I wonder if he can also make spats?
A helmet, would do for a man of the law,
I've listed some hats – it's the end of them all.

Betty Moir

YOUTH - AUGUST 1940

How bright the sun shone,
When we lazed
In the heat haze
Rising over 'The Plain'.

As we gazed
From under the dark verandah,
Full of hope, youth and fun
With our brand new gun
The war should soon be won.

So we sat in the sun
On a little mound
Of dusty ground
Cleaning hard wax-fat
From stock and bolt;
'Clatter-clatter-clack'
We are casing springs
When we get back
To civvi things
What a tale we'll tell
To many a girl?

The bugle sounds for pay;
There'll be rice pudding again today
And tomorrow the same, so they say
An endless progression thro' stodge.

But today we're young
And our summer's long
Tonight there's the pub
And a bawdy song
The bugle calls again:
'Today we polish . . . today we rub'
My webbing I shall have a scrub
Before we mount the guard tonight.

I met a lass at Tidworth Fair
With bright grey eyes
And auburn hair.
We lay together by a tree
But she will never wait for me.

How bright the sunshine,
In the morning sky
The lark soars high
Driving out dark

With her sweet cry
But we heed her not.
In hedgerows flowers gay
Blossom for the day
But we see them not.

There's no more fear
Nor noise to hear
We've neither pain
Nor hope of gain;
No love, nor joy
For any boy,
There's only the tread
Of the feet of the dead
That silently falls,
Instead.

Gordon Charkin

DES RES OR MOD CONS?

The Cotswolds, the Quantocks or a Derbyshire Dale,
By auction, by tender or 'houses for sale'.
A smuggler's hideaway, the Cornish coast,
A Sussex barn or a converted oast,
Devonshire cottage, cosy and thatched,
A 'desirable residence', or semi detached.
Pre-fab bungalow, jerry built,
Castle, mortgaged up to the hilt,
Croft in the Highlands – a real thrill,
Lonely, ancient, tumbledown mill.
Inaccessible, humble abode
For even the mail man without a postcode,
Luxury caravan, towed 4x4,
Swish 'mod cons' and all door to door.
High-rise apartments, or back room flat,
Suburbia or slum, I wouldn't mind that.
The address doesn't matter – on hill or in valley,
West End of London or 'Garbage pit alley'
Away from the world, I'll settle for this
As long as I'm with you, my life'll be bliss.

Ian Pulford

WHILE I LAY DREAMING

I had a dream
As young men do
A very special dream
With a picture of you
While I lay dreaming
You came into view
Is that dress you're wearing
Shimmering green or blue
And the song they're playing
They're playing specially for you
Those colours in the background
So many different hues
Your face, your hair
Your deep red lips
Are all so precious too
And your figure's
Unbelievable
That bewitching smile
Just sets my heart aglow
You really are so special
I can't believe you're true
So let me keep on dreaming
So I can know more about you.

Martin Selwood

VIRGINIA TREE

A tree planted in memory
Of me and Virginia Bailey
Met at Farney Close School in 1977
Made magic in Farney Woods such heaven
New headmaster in 1979
Stopped our magic making with a fine!
Lazy filthy parents at home
Shamed my teenage years alone
WDC and then 4 West
Exploited my labour for pocket money 'but'
All got in the way of our love
So in this tree our love is sealed
In years from now future folk will see
HGG still in love with VB!
Find it at Normanton le Heath
In Leics New Forest!

Hugh Griffiths

THE SHOCK

She said, 'Your job is on the line.'
The line? Why, there it was,
Just cracking open at my feet,
Brink of a bottomless abyss.
And there was I, no head for heights!
The shock fair made me reel.
The whole room spun around the mouth,
So dizzy did I feel.
Around the sympathetic mouth,
The room spun round and round,
Around the apologetic mouth.
I grabbed a chair and sat down.
The mouth was talking, talking still,
Explaining on and on
But all I heard and all I knew
Was that my job was gone.
Looking down I saw what soon must be:
Wide-eyed incomprehension,
The distress of my near relatives,
Family gloom and tension.
I saw myself a-dangling
From a bush on the ravine's side.
Desperate. Self worth in tatters.
Clinging undignified.
Ere long comforts would hurtle past,
Holidays, car, house and all!
Then I would follow to the depths.
Just how far down must I fall?
This vertigo would never stop
If I kept looking down
I must get off this nightmare,
This Hitchcockian merry-go-round.

But on the ring-of-roses turned
And mocking demons rhymed,
'Ashes! Ashes!
Your job is on the line!'

The kind mouth said, 'So, you see my friend,
Why your job is on the line.
You're rather pale. Are you alright?'
Smiling I said, 'I'm fine!'
For when the reeling stopped I heard
A still small voice divine.
'Fear not!' it said, 'I shall supply
Your needs, for you are mine.'

Valerie Archer

THE EQUINE LINE

He is one of the family
No, he's not your brother
He's regally majestic
One way or another
Withers, a hoof or a frog?
He drinks sup after sup
He can't be nailed down
But can be tacked up
Could be a sweet runner
Though he is not a bean
Maybe he's a chestnut
Best you've ever seen
Could be an Arab grey
That's all-right
Could be a coloured
Stable black and white
He'll never leave you
Mane man without fail
He eats like a horse
Thereby hangs a tail

William Brownlee

YARMOUTH ROAD - FEBRUARY 2004

Going home once more
Down familiar roads
With trees, like friendly faces
Standing on a street corner; bent and bony;
Stark as metal railings partly hidden
By electric cables and distant sheds
Where wild winter winds glide wingless
Into blind black corners and fain death
Like a crafty enemy.
And there as a child I ran free
Away from the sweating town
With its pointing chimneys and curves
Of industrial smoke;
And as the North Sea no longer
Battered and teased those wooden shoe
Boxes called drifters and trawlers
The town slowly died street by street
Neighbour by neighbour
Till I go from my place of birth
Untouched and unmoved as if it was a convenience meal
Free from natural flavour and colour, that seldom hits the spot;
Or is it because I am nearer autumn than spring?
And I have lived too long in the company of noisy strangers.
Each one kicking stones and slippery shingle in my over crowded mind.

Laurence DE Calvert

FORWARD POETRY INFORMATION

We hope you have enjoyed reading this book - and that you will continue to enjoy it in the coming years.

If you like reading and writing poetry drop us a line, or give us a call, and we'll send you a free information pack.

Alternatively if you would like to order further copies of this book or any of our other titles, then please give us a call or log onto our website at www.forwardpoetry.co.uk.

Forward Poetry Information
Remus House
Coltsfoot Drive
Peterborough
PE2 9BF
(01733) 890099